PRACTICAL
Tarot Techniques

Marcus Katz

Marcus Katz is a professional tarot teacher at the Far Away Centre, a contemporary training centre in the Lake District of England. As the Co-Director of Tarot Professionals, the world's largest professional tarot organization, he has studied and taught tarot for thirty years and has delivered more than 10,000 face-to-face readings. His first book, *Tarosophy*, has been termed a "major contribution" to tarot by leading teachers. Marcus is also the co-creator of *Tarot-Town*, the social network for tarot, with over 10,000 people worldwide sharing innovative tarot development.

Tali Goodwin

Tali Goodwin is the Marketing Director and Co-Founder of Tarot Professionals Ltd., the largest professional tarot organization in the world. She has co-authored innovative teaching books such as *Tarot Flip*, which is regularly in the top ten best-selling tarot books on Kindle. Tali is a skilled researcher and is credited with bringing the long-hidden Waite-Trinick Tarot to publication in *Abiding in the Sanctuary: The Waite-Trinick Tarot*. She also co-edited the leading tarot magazine, *Tarosophist International,* from 2010–11.

To Write to the Authors

If you wish to contact the author or would like more information about this book, please write to the author in care of Llewellyn Worldwide, and we will forward your request. Both the author and the publisher appreciate hearing from you and learning of your enjoyment of this book and how it helped you. Llewellyn Worldwide cannot guarantee every letter written to the author can be answered, but all will be forwarded. Please write to:

Marcus Katz & Tali Goodwin
% Llewellyn Worldwide
2143 Wooddale Drive
Woodbury, MN 55125-2989

Please enclose a self-addressed stamped envelope for reply, or $1.00 to cover costs.
If outside the U.S.A., enclose an international postal reply coupon.

PRACTICAL
Tarot Techniques

Your
Essential
Tool Kit
for
Better
Readings

Marcus Katz and Tali Goodwin

Llewellyn Publications
Woodbury, Minnesota

This book was previously published as *Tarot Face to Face* (2012).

FIRST EDITION
First Printing, 2019

Author photos © www.derwentphotography.co.uk
Book design by Bob Gaul
Cover art © Frame: iStockphoto.com/Heidi Kalyani
          Ornate rule and scrolls: iStockphoto.com/Angelgild
          Grunge Frames: iStockphoto.com/Pingebat
                    iStockphoto.com/Artur Figurski
Cover illustration: Eugene Smith
Editing by Lee Lewis Walsh
Interior tarot card art (reprinted by permission):
  Llewellyn:
    Gilded Tarot © Ciro Marchetti
    Legacy of the Divine Tarot © Ciro Marchetti
    Mystic Dreamer Tarot © Heidi Darras and Barbara Moore
    Revelations Tarot © Zach Wong
    Shadowscapes Tarot © Stephanie Pui-Mun Law and Barbara Moore
    Wizards Tarot © Corrine Kenner and John Blumen
  Lo Scarabeo:
    Universal Tarot © Roberto De Angelis
    Wheel of the Year Tarot © Maria Caratti and Antonella Platano
Interior illustrations © Llewellyn Art Department

Llewellyn is a registered trademark of Llewellyn Worldwide Ltd.

Library of Congress Cataloging-in-Publication Data
The Library of Congress has already cataloged an earlier printing under LCCN: 2012019117

Llewellyn Publications
A Division of Llewellyn Worldwide Ltd.
2143 Wooddale Drive
Woodbury, MN 55125-2989
www.llewellyn.com

Printed in the United States of America

Dedications

This book is dedicated to my son, Ricky Katz, who didn't get anything dedicated to him already because he was busy being Ricky Katz. It is also dedicated to my brother Graham, his wife, Kai, and my nephew and niece Ben and Abigail, who showed great patience during the final editing of this book.

—Marcus

This book is dedicated with love to my partner, Lyn Birkbeck, who shows me the path in the stars, and to the memory of Emma-Mary Birkbeck, whose unique engagement with life taught me so much face to face.

—Tali

Anistita Argenteum Astrum, the Priestess of the Silver Star, she whose light leads the way to the Arcanum Arcanorum, the Secret of Secrets.

Vos Vos Vos Vos

V.V.V.V.

Acknowledgments

We would like to acknowledge the support of all those friends and contacts on Facebook who stuck with us during the writing of this book, particularly students on our Hekademia 2-year Tarot course who found themselves suddenly without a principal teacher during the week in which we laboured to complete the manuscript.

And we would like to acknowledge HB and HM, for astral guard duties.

Contents

Introduction

During our tarot workshops, we have taught novices as well as the far more experienced tarot devotees who have immersed themselves in study of the cards. Many of these students have professional jobs such as psychiatrists, prosecuting attorneys, nurses, teachers, firefighters, and architects. We have found that tarot touches people from all walks of life and crosses all social barriers.

We never fail to marvel at how somebody who has no prior knowledge of tarot can progress quickly and attain a profound grasp of the craft of tarot through learning just a few simple skills. This book will teach you these skills, and more. One student, who had never held a tarot deck in her hands before, surprised us by giving a card interpretation with such authority and profundity that all those listening were left speechless. They could not believe that this student was totally new to the cards and had had only two hours of instruction. When asked about her seemingly effortless ability to read the cards, she wondered why it was that *we* thought it would be difficult—she had no assumptions at all, as she knew nothing about the subject.[1]

The moral of this story is that if you do not allow yourself to be frightened of or intimidated by tarot, it can be surprisingly easy to learn.

In this book, you will be getting face to face with tarot in encounters ranging from reading for yourself, to reading for friends at parties, to reading for complete strangers. You will learn ways to read the cards to answer all the questions you will ever ask or be asked, as well as how to incorporate tarot into your daily life.

Over the years, students have told us what really confuses them about reading the cards, what areas cause them to lack confidence, and which aspects of interpretation create the most difficulty. We're well acquainted with the common issues students experience when delivering their first readings face to face. You will reap the benefits of our decades of discovery and become a confident, accurate, and adaptable reader of tarot in any situation.

We aim for you to experience tarot in all its facets, showing you how to quickly and easily discover more about yourself and others, your relationships and the world, both mundane and mysterious, through this fascinating deck of images.

One

Face to Face with Your Deck: Essential Skills and Methods

The tarot serves us as a pack of possibilities, a divination of the divine, a dynamic reflection of the psyche, a search engine of the soul, a GPS of the spiritual journey, and a mirror of our dreams. In coming face to face with the seventy-eight images of a tarot deck, we are only coming face to face with ourselves.

We may be surprised, then, to see in those very depths the same heights our soul seeks, reflected endlessly in a single universal face—one with the seventy-eight diverse expressions of a tarot deck.

We have broken this first chapter into two sections, one dealing with the essential *skills* you need to perform great tarot readings, and the other the *methods* that apply those skills to greatest effect, by which these readings are performed. As professional trainers, we know that many people trying to teach tarot confuse these terms, and end up teaching lots of methods that students will find difficult in practice because they have not yet learnt the skills that are required for the method. At first, it may appear that these essential skills don't have anything to do with tarot. However, you will be amazed at how practicing them will give you a head start when you begin to study the methods that follow in the next section.

You can approach all the exercises and games in this book as an absolute beginner with no resources other than your tarot deck and your own ability to respond to pictures, or hand in hand with other tarot reference books, whichever you prefer. We suggest that you invest in a journal where you can make notes and respond to the exercises; it will provide a valuable reference to look back on as your skills progress.

We have also asked hundreds of tarot readers in our social network, Tarot-Town.com, what makes a good reader, and added that feedback into this chapter. You will be guided toward the best skills of the professional, no matter whether you are studying tarot as a beginner or working toward doing professional readings yourself. It is never too early to learn from some of the best readers in the world!

Essential Skills: Learning and Speaking the Language of Symbols

We are going to demonstrate that tarot is a language of pictures (or images, or symbols—here those terms all mean the same thing), and one that can be learnt in a variety of ways. However, before we start, we want you to commit to heart one key concept. Few people teach it and even fewer learn it, so we want to ensure you are already ahead of the game:

Every symbol can really mean anything at all.

Please reread that sentence a few times. It is the secret of how tarot works, how the world works, and how you will avoid wasting hours of your life arguing with people about what a tarot card *really* means. Of course, it is not quite as simple as that, but symbols are "multivalent"—they can carry a range of meanings. These meanings are dependent on one thing: context. Thus meaning is given to a tarot symbol by the

3 of Swords (Mystic Dreamer Tarot), 2 of Swords, Justice (The Gilded Tarot)

question that someone asks you, the deck you are using, the moment you're performing the reading, as well as your own experience, knowledge, and intuition.

It is also true that most symbols have accepted, commonly understood meanings. These are bound by our common perception of the world as human beings. For instance, most of us would understand the symbol of a broken heart—in tarot, represented by the Three of Swords.

However, until the concept of courtly love became known in the Middle Ages, the notion of a broken heart would have carried a far different interpretation—probably a more mundane, medical one!

So whilst it is useful to have at least one reference book of symbols and meanings to hand (see our suggested reading lists at the end of this book), we must not take these at face value. There is a skill that is important to learn first—that of *bridging*. Bridging can be defined as visually and/or intuitively connecting the symbols of the cards in a way that makes sense in the context of the reading.

When experienced tarot readers look at cards and symbols, they are able to make "bridges" of interpretation between the symbols. For example, they might tell the querent, "In this card (the Two of Swords) and in this one (Justice), we see a blindfold. The sword held by Justice tells me that the decision in your legal case will be reached soon and will be fair to you, even though you cannot see it at the moment." For some, this skill of bridging is a natural ability; for others, it can be gained from experience. Either way, it can be taught, and learnt, as a specific skill that will rapidly build your tarot-reading confidence.

Exercise: Bridging

In this example, we will use the Six of Swords and the Star.

Here's what we might say about bridging these two cards:

6 of Swords and the Star
(The Universal Tarot)

The Six of Swords shows a daytime background, while the Star is visible only at night. It would be great to be on a journey, as in the Six of Swords, with the Star card ahead like a guiding beacon. There is water in both cards, although it is being controlled more in the Star card. I get the general feeling that both cards have something to do with flow.

Now take two cards from your deck. Make a note in your journal or say out loud what you can see that bridges these cards. In other words, what happens in your mind when you see these two images together? Our minds are automatic sense-makers (and sense-breakers) in the processes we call language and learning. Images and symbols are part of that—in fact, you are doing it now to make sense of these weird black squiggle shapes on the page.

You can use comparisons, contrasts, themes, distinct symbols, colour, shape, form, numbers, or anything else that occurs to you. The important thing is not to try and interpret the cards, nor make sense of them individually. This is not what good tarot readers do at all, although it is the way tarot tends to be taught, unfortunately—one card at a time. (More on that later.)

Don't reject any thought that arises, whether it is a statement of fact or an intuitive impression—especially things that don't appear to make sense. Have fun and let your consciousness flow until you can't say or write anything more. The goal is to face the cards in a spirit of enquiry, so if you feel as if you are working too hard or having trouble, simply shuffle the deck and choose a couple of different cards.

Exercise: Pinpointing

The next skill is to intuitively locate the centre of an individual card— something we call *pinpointing*. This allows us to fine-tune our bridging to make it relevant to the individual cards laid down in a spread. Like bridging, pinpointing is something that experienced readers do unconsciously. We've used a technique called neuro-linguistic programming (NLP) to model how that happens, so we can teach it to you here.[2]

Pinpointing actually works better when more cards are laid out, and doing so also helps us get over the incorrect assumption that a spread with more cards is harder to read. So take five or six cards out of your deck and spread them out randomly across your table or workspace, face-up. Hover your hand over them with your forefinger pointing down. When you feel that you want to bring your finger down, place it on the physical centre of one particular card.

Now lift up your finger and take note of what you see in that location. It could be a symbol ("a belt buckle shaped like a lion") or one detail of a wider image ("a red colour, which is part of the hat of a young man").

Repeat this several times and see if you are often drawn to the same card. Take a break and then try the exercise again with different cards. Keep practicing it over a period of time, say a week.

Once you have a good feel for pinpointing the centre of one particular card, you can move on to the next part of this skill. Repeat the exercise, but this time, allow your finger to drop onto the "centre of meaning" of a card. That is, not the physical centre as before, but a part of the card that you feel drawn toward for its importance. This could be a major symbol ("the sun") or something quite minor ("a snail in the corner of the picture of a garden"). Make a note of this as before and take time over a few days to practice.

In doing this exercise, you are learning to make sense of a large amount of images by focusing your attention on meaningful parts. It is like picking up a language by listening to it being used, identifying specific words and phrases, and eventually making sense of them in context. The teaching of tarot in this book is an immersive experience in the world of symbols.

We are now going to practice our essential skills. Think of the scene in the movie *The Karate Kid*, where the student complains he has not been learning anything useful other than painting the fence and waxing the car. The master then demonstrates how these repeated motions are in fact the blocks and defences of karate, now perfectly practiced and ready for use. Let's see if this works for tarot. *Hai!*

Exercise: Practicing Your Skills in a Reading

Most tarot teachers go through the cards individually and gradually build up to doing readings over a period of weeks, sometimes starting with simple two- or three-card readings and then working up to larger spreads. This tends to result in students learning to read cards individually first, and then trying to make sense of them together afterwards, usually after a laborious crawl through every card in a spread as if it were the only card there. Once this has been learnt, it is hard to unlearn it. In addition to allowing you to practice your skills of bridging and pinpointing, this exercise will also help you get over the mistaken idea that more cards are harder to read—in fact, it can be quite the opposite.

Shuffle your deck. Randomly select twenty-five cards and lay them out, face-up, in a grid five cards wide and five cards tall. Cast your gaze over the cards, raise your hand, and *pinpoint* (you have the skill, like "paint the fence") one meaningful location. Then raise your hand again and pinpoint another. Next, consider those two symbols and *bridge* them ("wax the car"). Speak your ideas aloud or write them down in your journal.

When you have finished talking or writing, repeat the same process, pinpointing and bridging two different locations on the cards. You'll soon find how incredibly rich and textured this process is, and how much your interpretations already sound like an incredible tarot reading—even before we've studied any of the individual cards. Our next essential skill will teach you more about how to talk this walk, and then we can quickly move on to essential methods, which will seem incredibly easy to perform now that you have learnt the skills that lie beneath them.

You now have two very useful skills, *bridging* and *pinpointing*. When combined, they give rise to a third skill: *navigating*. Here, basically, we take our picture-appreciation from the previous two skills and apply it to talking about our cards. As with everything you are learning, this comes to experienced tarot readers over time. You are short-cutting years of experience to learn the skills that go into masterful readings, so that you can rapidly move beyond the basics and find your own voice.

Exercise: Dialogue with the Cards

When we read tarot, we have multiple dialogues—conversations—with our deck, our own inner responses, our client, and sometimes divine sources. Thus when we ask the cards a question, *imagining* a verbal response from each of these aspects allows us to more clearly identify the issues at hand and the underlying theme of the reading. A list of intriguing questions for practice can be found at the end of this exercise. As an example, we will ask the cards, "What is being created right now?"

*Knight of Pentacles
(Wheel of the Year Tarot)*

Shuffle your deck and turn up the first card. Our example card is the Knight of Pentacles.

Study the card, apply your new skill of pinpointing, and imagine the reply: "A world of plenty

5 of Wands, 10 of Swords, 8 of Cups (Wheel of the Year Tarot)

is being created, full of grapes that can be transformed into pleasure and joy. The world is created for us to recognise and grasp, and it brings us many messages from which to learn…"

Your imagined response can be drawn from the images on the card, such as the scrolls on the saddle that represent messages, your knowledge of the card's meanings, your own intuition, or all of the above.

Next, you have the choice of asking the deck another question, entering into further dialogue in response to this card by drawing another, or making your own statement.

You might say, "Well, that's all very interesting, but what about God's role?" Then pick the next card. Our example card is the Five of Wands.

As you apply your skills of pinpointing and bridging, you imagine the card's answer, "God is a light that shines down upon all our struggles on earth. And yet, at the same time, we are hand-in-hand with the divine, working for or against the flow…"

Let's continue the dialogue: "So you are saying there is a struggle?" We draw the Ten of Swords.

It replies, "There is indeed a struggle, against death and mortality. The raven sits and watches all things pass away in time. The moon is itself only a reflection of light, and in that illusion we mourn all our lost opportunities…"

You can see how easy it is to create a conversation. "Oh, well, that sounds bleak…" we say, and draw another card, the Eight of Cups.

The card says, "It is. We must walk away from whatever attracts us, for it is only an illusion that leads to sorrow. In our own journey through life, we must rise above our struggles to find the divine plan…"

And so on, for as many cards as the conversation requires. Have a good talk with your tarot—but hopefully not as solemn a conversation as the usually joyous Wheel of the Year Tarot deck gave us in our example.

Here are some additional thought-provoking questions to consider:

1. What sort of story is my life?
2. Where should I start on my path?
3. When the Universe talks, what is its tale?
4. What will the world (or humankind) grow into?

And here are a few for use with a brand-new deck:

1. How may I use you best?
2. What sort of friend are you?
3. What kind of magic are you?

Essential Methods: Using Key Phrases and Keywords

Having practiced our essential skills, we'll now learn the essential methods that will soon have you reading tarot easily and enjoyably.

Building on the previous exercise, we'll apply the concept of navigating—which, you will remember, is talking to and about your deck—to a basic method that has served our students well: the use of key phrases and keywords. Below are some examples of what you might actually say when reading each card. Both upright and reversed meanings are given. These key building blocks are drawn from our small reference book, *Tarot Flip*, which provides a self-contained guide to all seventy-eight cards. You can also refer to our work *Around the Tarot in 78 Days*, which takes the reader through the entire deck, building up methods and spreads including elemental dignities and the counting method.[3]

The Major Arcana

0: The Fool

Upright keyword: Frivolity

What you say: "Take a light-hearted leap into the unknown, for you are free!"

Reversed keyword: Seriousness

What you say: "The Fool doesn't stay upside-down for long. Before you know it, you'll be laughing about this situation!"

I: The Magician

Upright keyword: Success

What you say: "The Magician brings success and resources to your endeavours."

Reversed keyword: Failure

What you say: "The reversed Magician indicates that you do not have the required resources for what you wish to accomplish."

II: The High Priestess

Upright keyword: Revelation

What you say: "The High Priestess will reveal what is hidden."

Reversed keyword: Secrecy

What you say: "When reversed, the High Priestess tells us that something is being concealed."

III: The Empress

Upright keyword: Cultivation

What you say: "The Empress brings gradual growth to your life."

Reversed keyword: Harm

What you say: "The reversed Empress warns that harm may come about because of your intended actions."

IV: The Emperor

Upright keyword: Endurance

What you say: "The Emperor signifies power and endurance in your situation."

Reversed keyword: Instability

What you say: "When reversed, the Emperor shows instability in your situation."

V: The Hierophant

Upright keyword: Teaching

What you say: "When the Hierophant appears, he says that we must teach."

Reversed keyword: Learning

What you say: "When the Hierophant is reversed, we are being told we must learn."

VI: The Lovers

Upright keyword: Union

What you say: "The Lovers brings all things together."

Reversed keyword: Separation

What you say: "The Lovers reversed indicates separation."

VII: The Chariot

Upright keyword: Momentum

What you say: "The Chariot brings great forward energy to the event or undertaking."

Reversed keyword: Stop

What you say: "When reversed, the Chariot brings a full halt to your energies and projects."

VIII: Strength

Upright keyword: Action

What you say: "'Take action' is the message that Strength brings in a reading."

Reversed keyword: Rest

What you say: "When reversed, the Strength card shows a rest is called for, to establish a better relationship to your life."

IX: The Hermit

Upright keyword: Solitude

What you say: "The Hermit signifies solitude: time to be by yourself."

Reversed keyword: Companionship

What you say: "The exact opposite of being a Hermit is to seek out companionship, which is the message of this card when reversed."

X: The Wheel of Fortune

Upright keyword: Movement

What you say: "The Wheel means that everything that happens is connected, and it moves the situation forward."

Reversed keyword: Pause

What you say: "When reversed, the Wheel shows we must take a pause and regain our centre."

XI: Justice

Upright keyword: Accuracy

What you say: "This card, Justice, shows a fair response to the situation. You reap what you sow."

Reversed keyword: Mistake

What you say: "When upside-down, Justice can mean a mistake is being made."

XII: The Hanged Man

Upright keyword: Surrender

What you say: "It's time to let go and surrender to your highest principles."

Reversed keyword: Struggle

What you say: "You may have to struggle to ensure your viewpoint is seen."

XIII: Death

Upright keyword: Life

What you say: "The Death card shows transformation and new life in your situation."

Reversed keyword: Stagnation

What you say: "Reversed, the Death card suggests that everything will stagnate and rot in this situation."

XIV: Temperance

Upright keyword: Assessment

What you say: "When the Temperance card appears, it suggests we assess the situation in a balanced manner."

Reversed keyword: Overcompensation

What you say: "Reversed, Temperance can show that we are out of balance and overreacting to the situation."

XV: The Devil

Upright keyword: Withholding

What you say: "The Devil card in this reading means that not all has been released; something is being withheld."

Reversed keyword: Liberation

What you say: "The Devil, when reversed, is a card of release and liberation."

XVI: The Tower

Upright keyword: Acceleration

What you say: "The Tower never asks—it just happens. An acceleration of events will bring sudden change."

Reversed keyword: Fall

What you say: "When reversed, the Tower shows things crashing down in slow-motion."

XVII: The Star

Upright keyword: Enlightenment

What you say: "The beautiful Star card symbolizes the light of vision leading you to a better future."

Reversed keyword: Darkness

What you say: "When the Star is reversed, you must trust your instincts, as things are unclear."

XVIII: The Moon

Upright keyword: Ignorance

What you say: "The Moon card in your reading shows that some things are unknown. You must learn more to progress."

Reversed keyword: Knowledge

What you say: "When upside-down, the Moon indicates knowledge. It appears that you know everything you need to know about this question."

XIX: The Sun

Upright keyword: Demonstration

What you say: "The sun shines equally on everything, meaning that this part of your reading is bright and obvious. Good news!"

Reversed keyword: Concealment

What you say: "Like the sun behind clouds, when this card is reversed, it means that things are being hidden at this time."

XX: Judgement

Upright keyword: Awakening

What you say: "The Judgement card shows which part of your life needs awakening."

Reversed keyword: Sleep

What you say: "When reversed, this card means that you must let sleeping dogs lie."

XXI: The World
Upright keyword: Beginning
What you say: "The World brings new beginnings and the dance of life itself. A powerful and comprehensive card to empower your life."
Reversed keyword: Ending
What you say: "When reversed, the World maintains much of the same meaning, only signifying somewhat more of the ending of the old life prior to the beginning of the new."

The Minor Arcana

Rather than using key phrases, as for the major arcana, our method for the minor arcana uses keywords. These simple keywords were gained through listening to hundreds of tarot readers actually using the cards.

The Suits

Pentacles:	Resources
Swords:	Expectations
Cups:	Imagination
Wands:	Ambition

The Numbered Cards

Ace:	Seed
Two:	Organization
Three:	Activation
Four:	Application
Five:	Boundary
Six:	Utilization
Seven:	Reorganization
Eight:	Direction
Nine:	Rest
Ten:	Return

The Court Cards

Page:	Channeling
Knight:	Responding
Queen:	Connecting
King:	Demonstrating

2 of Wands
(The Universal Tarot)

The Two of Wands would be read as the "organization of ambition." This is reflected in the usual artwork of the card, which is often given the keyword "planning." Another stock phrase for this card would be "getting your ducks in a row"—in other words, arranging your affairs.

Essential Methods: Using a Spread

It is easiest to apply little bits of learning in simple exercises in order to build up to grander efforts, so we will first look at a very simple reading method—a spread that allows us to apply and practice our essential skills of pinpointing, bridging, and navigating.

This sixteen-card spread, called the Lightning Matrix, is a variation of an ancient Greek oracular method called the Book of Lightning. It uses only the sixteen court cards in what we call a "split deck" method, introduced in the book *Tarosophy* by Marcus Katz.[4] This method separates out different parts of the deck for more precise readings; for example, using just one suit, or using major arcana cards only.

We will use this spread to divine how a situation is operating at an energetic level, beneath what we consciously perceive. It is an excellent spread for reading for yourself, as it uncovers facets of the situation you might not be aware of.

Note that in this method we will be encouraging a lot of *vague* intuition on your part. We are not yet going to lay down hard and fast rules—that can come later. There is a great deal of scope for play and guesswork in this method, so don't be too concerned about doing it "right"—there's no such thing in face to face tarot, so let's make that clear now!

We have found that some people believe the court cards are somehow difficult, but here we will see that they are not. Whilst we will return later to our keywords for the court cards as given in the previous section, for this spread we are going to use a different set of keywords, given by Gérard "Papus" Encausse (1865–1916) at the turn of the nineteenth century. Papus was a man after our own hearts, as he liked to "boil down" his ideas of teaching and turn them into spreads and methods, and from the simple he derived the elegant. He was also fond of coming up with ways of learning and memorising simple rules for the cards.

In Papus's *The Tarot of the Bohemians*, we read that the court cards stand for a man, a woman, a young man, and a child.[5] These correspond to the concepts of—and here we have rephrased slightly for contemporary usage—creativity, union, conflict, and transition.

- King: Creativity (areas of creation, inspiration, making things, building)
- Queen: Union (relationship, agreement, coming together, mixing)
- Knight: Conflict (argument, friction, difference)
- Page: Transition (movement, change, communication)

Exercise: The Lightning Matrix

Take out the sixteen court cards, usually called page, knight, queen, and king. If you are using the Thoth Tarot deck or similar variants, you will discover these are called, somewhat confusingly, princess, prince, queen, and knight. We remember this alternate naming system by saying, "The princess is a page, the prince a knight, the knight a king, but at least the queen is always a queen."

Consider a situation or topic you wish to explore. This could be your relationship, employment, health, a house move, or a legal issue—anything, really, as long as it relates to *you*, not someone else. (Of course, we use our reading as just one factor in our decision-making, not as a substitute for professional advice on critical topics.) Our cards are trusted tools of insight and offer us new perspectives, perhaps even so accurately as to predict the most likely future—but for now, let's take them as new friends we do not yet entirely know or trust.

The situation can be as simple or complex as you wish. We never have a full picture of the map of the territory in which we live, so it really doesn't matter whether you focus on some general situation or a specific aspect of it. We choose a topic when reading tarot to assist with our interpretation, although in actual practice we often find the cards answering another question entirely, not the one that has been asked. When this happens, we go with what the cards seem to want to tell us.

Shuffle the cards. When you are ready, and this can be at any point, stop shuffling. Strangely enough, this is one of the most-asked questions in our classes and online—not "how do I read the cards?" but "how do I know when to stop shuffling?" Whilst it is an important question, since we all want to ensure the cards we lay out are the "correct" ones, the usual answer is the most annoying one: "You just know." We sometimes wait for a card to "stick" in place, or to feel as if they are being arranged just so. If you prefer a fixed method or rule, try shuffling as you recite a certain verse, prayer, invocation, or statement. An example might be, "O cards of power, in this hour, tell me true, tell me do." Repeat this verse for the magical number of seven times and then stop shuffling. You can also devise your own verse.

Lay out the cards, face-up, in four rows of four. As you probably know, some spreads have fixed positions, where each position in the spread has a meaning or a context in which the card is read. Other spreads are more freeform and use a linear storytelling method wherein each card is read as part of a loose narrative. Here we're using what is called in *Tarosophy* a "nonpositional" spread, where the cards themselves, rather than their positions, denote their meaning in the overall interpretation.

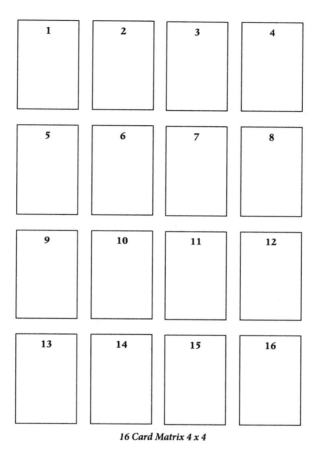

16 Card Matrix 4 x 4

Now that we have our matrix, cast your eye over the spread and see where your attention is *repeatedly* drawn. This may or may not be where your attention is *first* drawn. Think of it like walking into a crowded room and seeing patterns, such as noticing all the younger men or women first.

From our classes we know that not everyone is a visual person, so we have come up with useful alternative practices. If you feel unsure by just looking at the cards, try holding your hand palm-down and running it over the whole spread until you feel that one card is hotter, colder, sharper, or heavier than any others. If you feel this strongly, you are probably a kinesthetic person, rather than a visual one. You can also close your eyes and hum whilst imagining the whole square of the reading. Wait until your humming is interrupted in your head and then look to see which card corresponds with the "odd note" of your humming. It's like having radar go over the area until you get a "ping." If this works for you, you are likely an auditory person.

Now that you've identified the most significant card in the spread, we'll call it the *significator*. The word "significator" is from Latin, meaning sign—something that points to something else. It may seem strange to call one card the significator when every single tarot card in a reading points to some aspect of life experience in symbols. Usually, though, the significator is taken to represent the person asking the question. In this reading, the card you have repeatedly been drawn toward is *your* position or role in the situation we're exploring.

To interpret it, firstly consider the location of the card—is it in the middle? That simply means that you are in the centre of the situation—it is all about you! If your card is on top, this means you are looking down on the situation; in other words, you are somewhat removed from the main event. If your card is on the bottom, you may be feeling overwhelmed. Allow the feelings and impressions to come to the surface freely, and don't censor yourself.

Next, we see in our matrix where the energy is flowing. The energy of the court cards is very simple—king: creativity; queen: union; knight: conflict; page: transition. Take a look first at creativity—where is that shown in your matrix? Are there several kings together? Where are they located—a little creative hub in one area of the reading, or scattered all around? Keep in mind that kings may also represent inspiration, or making and building things, depending upon your question.

Now look at the queens, symbolizing union (relationship, agreement, coming together, mixing). How are they trying to bring together the energy in the situation? What do you think this might indicate? Again, don't worry if your impressions are vague at the moment. This is a practice method to get us thinking.

Next take a look at the conflict cards—the knights. If there are a couple of them close together, this will show you the source of the conflict, whether inside yourself or between the people in the situation. Use your intuition and allow the images on the cards to speak to you.

Finally, consider the pages, which relate to transitions (also movement, change, and communication). These show where movement is likely, where change is happening. Are they all in one place, or scattered? How are they grouped with the other court cards? What might this mean?

Now look at the matrix as a whole once more. What other patterns are present? Considering these other factors can enhance your interpretation, an idea that we'll explore in more detail later. Do not be overly concerned that you may not be interpreting your matrix correctly. We have only just started on our journey. The trick is to see how face to face tarot uses simple rules to generate patterns that work with your intuition.

Here are four possible scenarios based on this spread. In all of them, you can see how easily your intuition combines with the patterns of the cards to arrive at a conclusion.

1. If your significator was a page (a transition card) and all the other pages were on the other side of the matrix from you, with two kings (creativity) in between, what might this mean? Do not read the suits yet, just the levels of transition or change, separated by creativity.

2. If three knights (conflict) surrounded a queen (union) in one corner of the matrix, what might this signify if it were a relationship question? What might this signify if the question were about one's finances instead?

3. If you were examining your job, and the lightning matrix had a row of pages (transition) in the diagonal, ending in a queen (union), would this mean that you should stick to your present job or take a partnership offer to start a new venture?

4. If you were reading to locate a lost item, and there were two queens (union) together with your significator card above them, would this mean that the item had been lost underneath something, or would it mean the item had been put out of sight higher up, like on a closet shelf? Might it mean that you lost the item in the women's changing rooms, or in a car park?

This reading method will teach you an almost infinite number of ways to read from just sixteen cards, based on learning only four keywords—creativity, union, conflict, and transition. (We are sure Papus would be very pleased to see us all using his idea.) We have not yet discussed how we would add in the meanings of the suits, which will deepen this method. We feel it best to practice in "layers," introducing each new idea after previous ones have been practiced and experienced fully.

We have chosen this spread to present first because it introduces the most fundamental skill of all excellent tarot readers—pattern recognition. You may recognise this term from chess, where it is the mark of a grand master. The simple rules of chess produce a massive amount of variations, just like a tarot reading. It is by learning and practising the basic skills that the tarot master is created. When you become more adept, you will start to recognise patterns in the clouds, the stars, the movement of a person's hand. The world will become a living and open oracle and in that moment all will be revealed to you. This is the true secret of face to face tarot: we use it to come face to face with the divine universe.

Two

Face to Face with Your Deck: Practicing Tarot

We had the opportunity for nine of our tarot students to attend an evening party with us to give readings. Later on that night, all nine students took part in performing a tarot reading for one querent. It is rare that you get nine readers all performing the same reading for you at the same time.

This was a win/win situation for the querent and the students. The querent was really thrilled at having a reading done in this way because of the diverse input from the various readers. In turn, all the students felt confident that they had something unique to contribute to the reading as a whole, and they gained from having the support of their fellow students.

One thing we noticed is that, whilst each of the students had their own unique voice in the reading and one would think they would contradict each other, every insight actually added a new layer or perspective to the reading, supporting it and giving it depth.

The moral of this story is that the tarot is as deep as the people using it, and sharing your cards can be an incredibly rewarding and enriching experience.

Spreads for Fun and Practice

In this chapter, we will take the tarot skills we learnt in our first chapter and apply them in a range of great activities that are designed to get your tarot-brain engaged while creating new ways of thinking and seeing the world through the deck. These activities are based on an idea called "installation," which works on the simple principle that in order to practice something, you have to unconsciously organise resources in your mind in a particular way. So we have designed these games and exercises to install and activate particular skills that are essential to tarot, based on decades of observing experienced tarot readers. These are methods we teach in our personal classes worldwide, revealed here for the first time. Your confidence will increase as you realise how quickly these skills can be learnt and practised while having fun!

Exercise: The Narrative Method of Storytelling

We will start by practising and installing the narrative method, a particular style of leading tarot author and teacher Rachel Pollack. You are going to create a story using the cards.

To start, split your tarot deck into three piles containing the court cards in one, the majors in another, and the minors in the third. Shuffle each pile and set it down. Select cards from each pile, without looking at them first, to create your story. Take the first card from the court card pile. This is the hero (or heroine). What sort of character is he (or she) and what sort of life does he lead? Feel free to refer to the companion book to your deck, if you have it, or our key concepts for that card given in chapter 1 of this book.

The next card, chosen from the majors, is the call to adventure. What changes in the hero's life to start him on his journey? For example, if you draw the Tower, it would indicate a major and sudden disruption, while the Wheel of Fortune might mean a repeated wake-up call. Since no specific spread is associated with this method, lay the cards out in a line, face-up, or arrange them any way you like.

The next card, drawn from the minors, is the nature of the hero's refusal to go on this journey or engage with this event or opportunity. What does he do? How does he respond?

The next card, a court card (or you can select a major card, if you prefer) shows the hero's mentor. Who or what encourages him, teaches him, or provokes him to change, and how?

The next card, a minor, shows the first threshold that must be crossed to enter a different world. For instance, if it were the Nine of Cups, the threshold might be the hero feeling a little too pleased with himself.

Now choose three cards, each from any of the three piles, to indicate the tests, allies, and enemies the hero encounters in this new situation.

The next card, a major, shows the next threshold and the nature of the innermost cave—in other words, the secret heart of this story, a revelation, where the hero encounters the ordeal (select a minor or major card) and gains the reward (select a minor or major card). What is the ordeal? What is its reward?

The hero then takes the road back to the starting point (choose a minor card) and crosses a third threshold, experiencing a transformation or resurrection. The minor card tells us what this experience is all about and perhaps even how it happens in the story.

Finally, the hero returns home with a boon or a gift to bring to his previous situation. This is indicated by the final card, a major. What is it he learns or brings back from this journey?

This sequence is based on the archetypal hero's journey described by Joseph Campbell and recast in contemporary style for authors, playwrights, and screenwriters in Christopher Vogler's *The Writer's Journey*. Underlying the hero's journey is a universal story pattern, the monomyth. All our lives partake of this mythical structure that is revealed in our stories and creative acts. You may find that this spread reveals a lot about your own life story.

This method illustrates how we can utilise the cards in specific ways to creative dramatic narratives: the majors are archetypal forces at play, the minors the events in everyday life manifesting those forces, and the court cards the characters. Whilst practising creating stories in this manner, you are also unconsciously learning ("installing") a new sense of how the cards represent these same elements in a spread for divination. You should find your ability to read cards progressively increasing and deepening as you practice this exercise.

Exercise: Doubt and Anti-Doubt

Next, we will look at a simple way of facing up to your daily doubts in an exercise designed by Tali. This useful technique works with self-selecting tarot cards and then adds a little twist.[6] It helps you accept, face, and resolve your doubts, particularly any self-defeating ones at the start of the day.

First, grab hold of your doubt. Hold it closely, really wallow in it; be certain that you have the doubt well and truly in your sight. This is the first trick and may seem counterintuitive, since most people try to push doubts to one side or take a "positive thinking" approach. We prefer

7 of Pentacles
(The Revelations Tarot)

always to start from a real position, embrace it, and then use tarot to transform it. We're all for the real!

Next, think about which tarot card most closely matches your innermost doubts. Go through your deck and choose a card that reflects your most significant concern of the day. Select several cards if you feel like it, and then choose one that stands out the most.

As an example, Tali chose the Seven of Pentacles—a plateau reached, but still the goal is not attained. At this stage we can be very hard on ourselves, especially when we have worked hard to achieve what we have created so far, but have doubts that it is good enough. We may worry about what others will think, since we tend to measure ourselves against the achievements of others.

Now, think about which tarot card most closely matches your strengths. Go through the deck and select a card that matches one of your strengths or your experiences. It does not have to be connected to the doubt of the day. Choose a card that represents something real and true about yourself. Here we are more interested in the state of certainty (which is a step toward anti-doubt) than the context.

Tali's example card was the Eight of Pentacles. Here it denotes that she is certain she has the drive to keep working and creating in order to arrive at the end result. She has a strong work ethic and sense of pride in the work at hand, a determination to get the work completed to the best of her ability. She also has experiences in her life that reflect this strength, so she is happy to choose it as a real card that means something to her.

8 of Pentacles
(The Revelations Tarot)

Now that we have these two cards, one for doubt and one for certainty, we can call upon a divinatory moment to connect them. This is the real magic of creative tarot.

The anti-doubt card is the bridge between doubt and certainty. To find your anti-doubt card, shuffle the rest of the deck whilst thinking about and accepting all of your doubts—even the doubt that you can apply your certainty card to the situation! Be honest with yourself; this is the only place you have that freedom. Then draw a card from the deck.

Place this card between the two cards already selected. It shows you who you must be, or how you must be, to ensure that the doubt is resolved today.

Tali drew the High Priestess, which relates to intuition, the subconscious mind, and that which is hidden. It tells her that she must trust herself and her abilities.

The High Priestess
(The Revelations Tarot)

Now for the twist, which compensates for the fact that sometimes we doubt our cards as well as ourselves. Turn the tarot deck upside-down and look at the bottom card. This tells us what to look for today as a sign that our anti-doubt is working.

Tali found the King of Pentacles at the bottom of her deck. This says she should look for all aspects of the King of Pentacles in any way during her day. She should also look for the "loyalty of other people" and "financial ideas and partnership" (see keywords in *Around the Tarot in 78 Days*). In doing so, she will unconsciously and magically be resolving her doubt and drawing on her strength, without having to do anything other than adjust her attitude. Her attention will be directed by the tarot to what she needs, and the Universe will do the rest.

Exercise: Finding Your Tarot Voice

In chapter 1, we briefly touched on the skill of speaking to and about your cards. Since we have found that many beginning students have trouble accessing their "tarot voice," we've designed this technique to "trick" it out of you. It works by overloading the conscious part of your brain's language center, so that you can easily access—or more accurately, easily let out—your unconscious voice. This has deep roots in your unconscious processes and hence is more amenable to intuition and rapid connection-making in your readings.

King of Pentacles
(The Revelations Tarot)

Choose a piece of music that has a lot of variation, which you feel comfortable listening to. It should be something that puts you easily into a state of dynamic relaxation, a piece that sounds like a powerful river—strong, yet flowing and in constant movement. Marcus uses *Californication* by the Red Hot Chili Peppers, but upbeat music from any genre will work equally well. Play the music at a volume that is clearly audible but not overwhelming.

Choose twenty cards at random and lay them out, face-up, in a row so you can see them all. Start to speak out loud, describing what you see on the cards, in either a literal or a symbolic way. As you speak, use linking words and keep the pace as rapid as possible. Here are some common linking words: and, so, when, whilst, because, then, where, or, if.

The aim is not to speak in orderly, complete sentences, but rather to keep the words flowing quickly, without censoring yourself. If you have trouble getting started, turn up the music a bit louder, till it nearly drowns out your voice. This helps to overcome your inner censor.

At some point, you may find yourself overtaken by sentences and words that are not in your conscious control, and appear to arise out of a deeper part of yourself. This is an unmistakable experience when it happens; the first time it does, you may suddenly startle yourself out of it. However, learning to access and trust this deeper intuitive voice is key to giving insightful, intuitive tarot readings. You can (and will) learn to get out of your own way.

Here is an example:

I see a woman holding a bird by a pool and there is a symbol of Venus and I can see lots of flowers and the woman wears a sash so I guess she is very rich because there are lots of coins in the archway there are tulips that probably come from the garden and the coins are now in a box where there are gemstones too which reflect the light because that has a key with some symbols on it and the light is also shining on the forehead of the priestess who is holding a scroll and a pomegranate and the archway is now two pillars as it is night and when the nighttime comes the hawk becomes the owl.

All of a sudden, the phrase "when the nighttime comes, the hawk becomes the owl" comes out of our mouth, and we stop and realise that

9 of Coins, 10 of Coins, The High Priestess (Legacy of the Divine Tarot)

we have just uttered our first oracle, because we have no immediate idea where that came from or what it means. However, our unconscious mind knows, and it brought that phrase to our attention for a reason. Now it's up to our conscious mind to figure it out.

Based on the cards involved, it could mean that the person for whom we are reading (or even ourselves if this was a reading for ourselves) has reached a "stuck" position with their material existence and must now somehow transform themselves in the darkness of their situation. Instead of being a hunter like the hawk, they must become more wise and patient, like the owl. It may symbolize a shift in their priorities, from the material to the more spiritual. You can ponder other ways of interpreting this oracular phrase.

Once we start to release this inner oracle, we may find our critical mind—our conscious, thinking mind, sometimes called the inner critic—starts to rebel and overanalyse. This is, of course, its job. In face to face tarot, we do not turn away from or attempt to frustrate this tendency; instead, we learn to harness it as a natural feature of our thinking. To do so, we must become aware of how our mind actually works.

We all have an inner, positive, "knowing" voice that guides us. In tarot, this would be represented by the High Priestess card, the deep intuitive part of us that actually lays down the law, which is often depicted as a scroll of Torah (law) on the priestess's lap. However, this guiding voice is often overpowered by negative thinking, old habits, and even the inwardly projected voices of significant others in our life, particularly our parents—this becomes our inner "criticizing" voice.

This critical voice, which judges us and finds us lacking, is very useful when we are looking to guide ourselves to continual improvement in a tangible skill, such as playing an instrument or a sport. But it is almost entirely useless when we seek to understand and improve a non-tangible skill, such as learning to read tarot cards. It sometimes seems as if the inner critic does not understand that one rule of life is constant change—the Wheel of Fortune card in tarot—and sometimes, astonishing and sudden change, like the Tower. So we had better learn to harness our inner critic and let it pull us, steer us, and guide us, rather than devour us.

Exercise: Harnessing the Inner Critic

For the following exercise, take the Strength card, the Chariot card, and the Judgement card from your deck and lay them out, face-up, in a row. The most common illustrations of the first two cards show the woman and the lion facing each other, and the charioteer facing us— and the world—directly and head-on. In the Judgement card, we face the very highest angel of our own spirit, the last and only true judge of our soul's progress.

Step 1: Perform a planned reading for someone, or a planned event. For example, you may be giving your first talk on tarot to a new group.

Step 2: When you have completed the experience, write down in your journal a totally positive assessment of how it went, highlighting only the good points—and do it in the third person. That is to say, write it like you are writing about someone else:

Marcus did well to get to the event on time, and most of his material was adequately prepared. He answered one question with good facts that he had learnt ahead of time. He had one person tell him that his diagrams were very useful.

Notice that this doesn't tell us anything about how "terrible" the rest of the event might have been. The first important thing is to tame the inner critic through the Strength card and enter into a right relationship with it whilst staring down the frightful jaws of the lion. This is completely contrary to what most of us have been taught. We are usually taught at school by a correcting principle—we are told what we have done wrong and are expected to improve as a result. We're told we have "only" scored a "low" 35 percent on a test, for instance, rather than something more supportive, such as, "You've made a good start and know 35 percent of the material so far. Well done."

Step 3: Now we take on the Chariot and see how we might improve. This is also done in third person, as if we were talking about someone else:

A person who had given a talk like that would benefit most by slowing down in his delivery and pausing to ask questions. He would likely get a better sense of the audience's comprehension and reduce extensive questions at the end by breaking the presentation into smaller sections.

This is harnessing the inner critic to provide helpful solutions, driving forward like the Chariot, as if we have taken the lion of the previous card and turned it into one of the sphinxes pulling our chariot. Note that there is no specific, *personal* criticism—we are using the inner voice in a removed sense to allow us space for creativity and positive solutions.

Step 4: Finally, we take a totally removed viewpoint, that of the angel in the Judgement card, looking down on all three positions (yourself, the positive critic, and the helpful critic). Here we summarize the situation:

Having heard that the material was well prepared, and that a talk like that could be made better by slowing it down, I judge that covering less material would be something to try for next time. This would ensure that the one giving this talk would have more space to provide question and answer sessions, breaking up the overall presentation and making it less like a lecture. I would also judge that the presenter should introduce a couple of linking games or exercises to ensure the audience understands the material.

This technique is used a lot in training games, and is a helpful way to get out of the old patterns of negative thinking and useless self-judgment. It works to break the old patterns by forcing a simple change in language, and is a great way of journaling too, particularly to make rapid improvements in your tarot readings. When next you undertake any of the exercises in this book, journal them using these three cards, and learn to harness the inner critic.

Exercise: Getting to the Detail

Another obstacle that beginners and even more experienced readers can face is getting to the detail of a reading, particularly when a querent has asked a very specific question. It can become a difficult situation when the reader is rambling on about the Hermit's lamp shining brightly across the two wands in the opposing card, when the querent simply wants to know whether to accept a local job offer or travel abroad.[7]

With this exercise, we will learn how to get a definite answer to any question by focusing on different details from the same three cards: The Initiate, the Two of Wands, and the Three of Pentacles. The practice of this simple technique will install a good "detail machine" in your head. It will also install a powerful unconscious model, which is that the cards are infinitely rich in detail and can be successfully applied to any question that you will ever be asked. Having this experience will automatically give you more confidence in reading—so practice!

The question: Whether to pursue an opportunity to go into business with a close friend, or do it by yourself.

The answer: Do it by yourself. Keep the friend as a consultant or standby, but do not involve him or her in the business.

The Initiate, 2 of Wands, 3 of Pentacles (The Wizards Tarot)

The detail: The Initiate is unsure; however, she has a companion to hand, for luck. The character in the Two of Wands keeps the "hot potato" of the new business slightly out of his hand; however, the other hand (the friend) is entirely empty. In the Three of Pentacles, the main character holds tightly to his pentacle, even though others may have their own pentacles to offer.

• What detail would suggest holding back any immediate and significant investment in the business?

The question: A romantic relationship at work appears to be developing; however, the querent is unsure as to whether there will be repercussions later.

The answer: The relationship will be insecure and constantly in the spotlight, so will not amount to a long-term, stable situation. It is mainly the secrecy of the relationship that is the draw, not anything long-lasting.

The detail: The Initiate card shows signs of untested experience—the "fluffy bunny," the vaporous smoke, the changing moon. The ten apples symbolise "forbidden fruit," indicating that the drama of the relationship is of more interest than the actual reality. The Two of Wands features two fires; however, they are burning separately, and one of the character's hands is empty, indicating imbalance or a one-sided relationship. The Three of Pentacles shows the constant observation of two elders who represent bosses at work; the character has to look over his shoulder.

• What detail would show reluctance from the other person in the relationship?

The question: The querent wants to know where she can find the inspiration and energy to write and finish a novel. However, conversation reveals that she's never even had articles or short stories published.

The answer: She needs to find a mentor and perhaps an agent who will encourage her, very forcefully, to develop a writing plan with strict deadlines.

The detail: The Initiate card shows the querent looking in her bag, from which a glow represents creativity. However, the same detail as in the prior question shows that her aims and ambitions are wispy. The Two of Wands shows another person holding the creative fire in balance, weighing it up constantly, symbolizing a writing plan and structure. In the Three of Pentacles, we see the apprentice being mentored by two people.

• Getting down to precise detail, what images would indicate whether the agency would be, say, one of these two: "The Monolith Agency" or "The Stars Agency"?

Here are some additional questions for you to answer by using these same three cards. All of them require only simple answers that may come either from one or two details or many aspects of the cards. You may like to share these with other readers and see if you all come up with similar answers.[8]

1. I am going on a three-month trip. Will I meet someone special?

2. There is a lot of turbulence going on in my career. Will I keep my job?

3. My court case has been extended and my lawyer advises I give in. Should I?

Note that this third question is about a legal issue, and of course a card reading is not a substitute in any way for legal or any other professional advice. However, a reading may provide invaluable insight not otherwise obtainable, and we have many tarot clients who are lawyers, doctors, consultants, and other professionals.

Creating Unique Spreads and Other Tricks of the Trade

Many of the spreads and methods here were designed spontaneously, in real time, with a querent asking a specific question, which we then turned into a customized spread. This is an extremely useful skill to develop. It's not as intimidating as it may sound, and once you get the hang of it, you will effortlessly create your own unique spreads for use in a wide range of situations.

Turn a Question into a Spread with Clean Language

In this example, the querent asked a question that was framed as, "I have two options, both of which are possible. One is probably more desirable than the other, but maybe I could do both. They're both a little bit out of my hands." Whilst he was asking the question, he was motioning with both hands in circular motions. This was intended to express his own unconscious model of how the two situations were moving and related to each other.

Marcus suggested using the classic "whirlpool" method[9] (sometimes called a "ripple spread"), which shows the ramifications of a particular choice or choices, and how these choices are interconnected. He first laid two cards down to show the essential nature or source of the two situations. Then he placed a ring of three cards around each of the two source cards to indicate how that particular situation would ripple out. Finally, he placed a ring of six cards around each choice to show the final outcome. At that point, the two rings had expanded on the table to overlap each other, with two cards, one from each situation, touching each other. The querent pointed these out and said, "I suppose this is what happens if I try to do both—they'll interfere with each other."

Marcus nodded and said, "Yes, so let's look at what happens in that case." At this point, he began to use a simple technique to clarify the actual, underlying issue. This technique is modified from the method of "Clean Language," based on the work of the late David Grove, a therapist in New Zealand.[10] Clean Language can be defined as a technique to clarify a situation through the use of metaphorical language, designed to minimize the impact of a person's conscious interpretations or assumptions.

In other words, when someone expresses his or her question, it usually has emotional content, which can be turned into a helpful metaphor using a specialized but straightforward series of questions. It only takes a minute or two, and then you have a precise metaphor for the question, against which to design your spread in real time.

The sequence of questions is as follows, with the essential word choices indicated in italics:

Reader: Please restate your question.

Querent: I have two options and I'm concerned that I may not make the right choice. (Note the emotional content of the querent's phrasing.)

Reader: So you're concerned. *Where is* your concern?

Querent: I don't really know. In my head. (The querent may also gesture unconsciously.) Reader: In your head. *Is it outside or inside?*

Querent: Inside, in my head.

Reader: Inside your head. I'm wondering how you'd best *describe the shape or size of that?*

Querent: Well, it's just everywhere and it's rushing about.

Reader: Rushing about? And *what is that like?*

Querent: It's like a bull in a china shop, really.

So now we have a metaphor, a bull in a china shop. You can then design a spread based on that concept.

You can frame the questions in any particular way, echoing the querent's own language. The faster you do it, and the more you pay attention to his or her whole communication, including nonverbal gestures, the more noticeable it will be that the question suggests its own spread in response.

The Bull in a China Shop Spread

The querent has asked whether to take an early retirement. He has described how his worries are rushing about like a bull in a china shop. We take the symbols of *bull* and *china shop* to quickly lay out a reading:

The Bull cards: What is it that drives the querent? Lay out three cards, face-up.

The China Shop cards: What will the querent gain or lose from taking early retirement? Lay out three cards, face-up, around the Bull cards.

The Outcome card: What will be the final outcome? Lay out one card, face-up.

You may also use any other variants that may strike you at the time of the reading, or as the querent explains his question, or as the cards are laid down. In this approach, we are using our intuition to be more responsive to the question in our divination, rather than forcing the question into a predetermined spread. It allows us to be more flexible and promotes an active dialogue with the deck, as well as a more engaging experience for the querent.

Turn a Word into a Spread

If you are performing e-mail readings, you can use a keyword in the querent's question to design an elegant and relevant spread. Here is an example:

Hello, I am asking about my relationship. I have been married for one year and we are discussing having children. I would like to have a reading because my parents used to say I was too irresponsible to have children and I want to know how my future might be if I do.

Here we would take that highly emotional word, *irresponsible*, as the main concern in the question. We then look up the etymology of the word in a dictionary or online source. We learn that "irresponsible" comes from "not responsible," and "responsible" comes from similar ideas like "obligation." The word "obligation" comes from the Latin and means "to bind." This of course leads to its later use as meaning "to make someone indebted by conferring a benefit or kindness."

We take the concepts of indebtedness and kindness and turn them into questions for a straightforward linear spread as follows.

1. What debt does the querent owe her parents?
2. What kindness did the querent learn from her parents?
3. What binds the querent in her attitude toward children?
4. What benefit will the querent be able to give to her children?
5. What responsibility will the querent take on?
6. What kindness will her child(ren) bring to her?

You can of course build upon those questions as the cards are placed and you engage in conversation with the spread itself. This can be a very powerful method because it takes much of the expectation for the reading out of your hands and places it, from the querent's question, directly in dialogue with the cards themselves. Your job is simply to interpret the reading.

Getting a Card to Fit a Question

We have already seen how you can apply any detail on a card to interpret a large range of questions that may be asked. We will see later just how many questions you will face as a tarot reader, and lots more ways of responding to them.

No matter what card is placed in which position of a spread, an experienced reader is able to interpret its meaning starting from basic keywords and concepts. However, this can often be difficult for those new to tarot. For instance, how does one apply a card whose keyword is "trespass" to a question about one's college exam?

We will use a method called "chunking," which describes levels of detail applied to thinking. Some people chunk in little details and others like to get the whole picture. Which one are you? If you are a "detail chunker" then you like to read the small print; if you are a "big picture chunker" you don't need details, you just want to know the overall shape of an idea. Often when an extreme detail chunker and a big picture chunker come face-to-face, it can cause all sorts of communication issues. A model of lateral thinking shows how people chunk in a particular unconscious strategy to solve problems in a creative way. We have applied this model to "making a card fit," as follows.[11]

In a question about a relationship, the Three of Wands showed up in the "past" position of a spread. This card has the keyword "building" and the key phrase "activation of ambition" (see the section on keywords in chapter 1). To make this fit, we need to look at the context (or metaphor) in which building makes sense to the question. Thus we can compare building a house to building a relationship. Obviously, setting the foundation comes early on in the process. So we then apply this to a relationship, perhaps seeing that the relationship was "cemented" in the past, based on the person's high ideals for the union. Those "foundations" are now in the past, denoting that the building has been completed and the relationship has moved on.

In another example, the Six of Wands was laid in the "advice" position of a particular spread. This card has the keyword "weariness." In the context of a question about entertainment, we would fit it into the reading by saying the querent is advised not to treat the situation as a game, otherwise he or she will tire of it.

Facing Up to Tricky and Slippery Cards

In the early days of a reading career, every reader comes to dread seeing certain cards turn up on his or her table. Of course, these cards then seem to turn up more often. It is almost as if certain cards know they spark some reaction in us.

A typical example is the Hanged Man, a card that Marcus had difficulty with for some years. It was almost as if something was in the card that he just could not get. When it turned up in readings, he would talk about the usual ideas of "suspension," "hanging around," and so forth. However, one day he was looking at the card after teaching a therapy class on values. He suddenly saw in the card that the Hanged Man was only fastened to one thing—the tree above. This could be seen as his values—that which supports him.

The Hanged Man can often be found in a situation where one must hold to one's highest principles and values, even where these seem upside-down and at odds with the world. This is why the Hanged Man appears to be content: he is being entirely true to himself. To him, perhaps the world is upside-down. Further, Marcus realised that every person sees the world through his or her own deep values, and is a projection of those same values. In other words, we see what is most important to us and automatically filter out everything else. Thus we can see that the Hanged Man is a lower version of the Hierophant, someone whose values are absolute and who reveals them fully.

For Marcus, this whole series of thoughts was catalysed by the singular concept that "the Hierophant is revelation, and the Hanged Man is the sacrifice required to receive that revelation. This is initiation."

Once you have had an experience like this with a slippery or tricky card, you will never forget it. So do keep broadening your reading, and your experience, and returning to the cards regularly. Their mysteries will continually unfold for you.

Exercise: Taking the Card Outside the Box

In this exercise, you will learn a method to confront a slippery card face to face and "trick" it into revealing more about its nature and its interpretation in a reading. These seemingly strange questions are taken from a Surrealist technique, "Exquisite Corpse," which is one of many such games in the Surrealist movement that can be applied to tarot to take it to whole new areas of thought.

- What might the card's profession be, other than the one it has?
- Is it happy or unhappy?
- What illness does it call to mind?
- With which historical figure can it be associated?
- How would you kill it?
- What question does it ask?
- What is its favourite song?
- Is it capable of change? How so?
- Does it believe in life after death?
- Is it capable of walking away from an argument?
- Does it come back when you don't care about it?

As an example, we might ask the Page of Swords from Ciro Marchetti's *Legacy of the Divine Tarot* these questions and receive the following answer:

I am a professional scholar, although I am just starting out. I can be very independent and critical in my work. I am unhappy, as people never understand why I need to be so ruthless to get to the truth of a matter—I just want to gain clarity. I have headaches. I am often seen as the new Kant or even Plato, although I prefer to be associated with

Page of Swords
(Legacy of the
Divine Tarot)

the symbolic logic of Charles Dodgson, better known as Lewis Carroll. I can be killed by being ignored or told to shut up, particularly when I ask my favourite question, "What does it mean?" I like the music of Kraftwerk and am always looking to what the Japanese call kaizen, *continuous improvement. I do not believe in anything; there are only ever the facts. I only walk away from an argument after I have won it. I don't really care about you, and I never come back.*

There are some surprises in this; we had never really considered how mechanical and predictable the Page of Swords can be, and this is beautifully illustrated in the music of the German electronic band, Kraftwerk. In fact, one might summarise the card as *"Vorsprung durch Technik"*—advancement through technology.

In this chapter we have seen how we can "install," or learn, different methods in order to create an entire tarot-reading system. In the following chapter, we will investigate the questions we will be facing in our tarot reading, asked either by ourselves or by others. We will then look at many different ways of responding to these questions in a range of situations.

Three

Facing
the Questions

There is a power at work beyond our wildest dreams when it comes to a tarot question that needs to be asked and needs to have some sort of resolution. There will be querents who are burning to speak their question but feel too stuck and frightened to voice it. We encountered one such querent who had been through a really traumatic time in hospital with an emergency medical situation. She had been told by her surgeon that it was a miracle she had survived the emergency and its complications. She had also experienced a really dramatic spiritual epiphany during this time. Following her recovery, she wanted to know why she had survived, and she still needed to come to terms with the long-term complications of her illness.

This woman was so driven by her burning desire to know why she had survived that she felt compelled to come along with her friend to our get-together for a tarot reading. However, when it was her turn to have a reading, she was so fearful she could not do it.

By the end of the night, she still had not had the reading. We were getting ready to go when her friend came to us and asked if we could manage to fit in her friend before we left. She explained her friend's strong need to have a reading but her equally strong fear—the woman was physically shaking with it.

We reassured her and explained to her what the tarot reading was all about before we started. She finally allowed us to proceed. Then gradually, card by card, the reading revealed revelation after revelation for her. We thought she would be pleased, but she still felt that her question was not being answered. We knew that she needed confirmation that there is something miraculous at work in our lives at all times, even though we do not understand why. It was then that Marcus felt compelled to say he thought Tali could help bring clarity to her question. Tali had undergone the very same medical emergency and survived against all odds. Even more surprising was that the surgeon had said the same thing to both Tali and the woman, and they both now had the same ongoing medical condition. Tali would normally never share this with anyone, but she felt moved to do so, since synchronicity was very much at work.

The moral of this story is that questions are there to be asked, so ask them!

———

In this chapter, we will ensure that as a reader you can handle every question with grace, inspiration, and accuracy. We will also cover methods to ensure your readings are relevant to the querent. To do so, we will be drawing upon some eighty thousand questions we have surveyed from online reading systems, for the first time revealing the types of questions asked of readers, the most frequent questions, and the most unusual, heartbreaking, or humorous. You will find yourself confronted by this incredible range of possibilities as a card reader, so this chapter will quickly increase your confidence and give you the equivalent of decades of experience.

Every Question Under the Sun—
and Every Answer

Given the range of our issues as human beings in a complex world, it is impossible for us to here give every possible response to questions you will encounter. Also, your own style will attract different questions from our own. Someone in the therapeutic community once commented that therapists get the clients they deserve; perhaps this is the same for tarot readers.

Similarly, your question base will be affected by your particular locale in space and time. During times of economic uncertainty, many questions will be about work and career choices; at the start of the year, questions will be about the year ahead; around Valentine's Day, questions will be about relationships.[12] In terms of your geographic location, the issues facing an urban audience will differ from a rural audience. In general, the urban audience will want to know about choices from many opportunities, while the rural audience will want to know how to get the most from more limited opportunities.[13] So here are some common questions and situations you may face, and our suggestions for dealing with them.

When the Querent Doesn't Have a Question

It is great when a person has a specific question; for example, "How will my new job work out?" or "Do you see a new relationship in my future?" However, often a person will sit down at your table and simply say, "Can you just do me a general reading?" or "I don't have any particular question, so let's see what comes up." Whilst this is perfectly adequate, you might want to explore whether there is anything more specific the client might wish to ask. You can do this through the use of creative questions.

Simply prompt the querent with the question, "If you were to wake up in the middle of the night tonight, what issues might be on your mind?" You can also ask, "If you were daydreaming whilst looking out the window on a pleasant day, where would your mind wander?" Questions like these can open a conversation that will sometimes bring up deeper and more important questions than the querent may have originally thought to ask. You may also ask if the person suddenly was visited by herself—from ten years in the future—and only had one minute to ask any question, what would it be?

You get the idea: we want to engage the querent's imagination. Feel free to come up with your own similar questions. Of course, most people will joke about wanting winning lottery numbers, or horse races or sports match results; keep your sense of humor, continue light conversation, and wait for the deeper questions to emerge.

Too Many Questions

At the other end of the range is the querent who gives you a whole barrage of questions; for instance, "Well, I have this new job and I've moved house but I haven't made any new friends yet and my father is ill at his home but that's just complicated because there's a vacation coming up and we have still got to settle the court case ... oh, and my cat is acting strangely, too." You can easily be forgiven for wondering where to start!

We have borrowed some useful tricks from counselling language for this situation. One is to first define priorities and relationships. The cat may well be reacting to the house move or the querent's stress—or both!—but is undoubtedly less of a priority than the father who is ill. Another trick is to listen for the word "just." This is a language marker for the "edge of belief," when someone's conscious and unconscious mind are interacting. As an example, when you say, "I just can't help myself," you are indicating that you are conscious of the behaviour, but not conscious of why you are repeating it—a factor that is unconscious. We use the word "just" all the time, and now that you know this, you will notice it more in conversation or when you read it.

So let's have another look at the long barrage given above by our "complex" client. Now you can see that the heart of the situation, the bit where conscious and unconscious motivation meet, is indicated by the word "just"—"just because there's a holiday coming up." In fact, the unconscious has already recognised this is the main issue, because it has placed in that part of the sentence the word "complicated."

So whilst it may be a surprise to the person, given what else they have offered us, we would say in response to this barrage, "I know this may seem an odd place to start, however, I want to consult the cards first on your behalf with regard to the vacation." We would then either ask the person to come up with a specific question about the vacation, or simply read for it as a situation and work from there. The fascinating thing is that this will rapidly uncover and untangle all the other issues at work—often in surprising and powerfully profound ways. The conscious mind may present complexity, but the unconscious will always signal the way into the issue through the word "just."

Another helpful trick is to listen for the phrase "it's like…" or, combined with the above, "It's just like…" This gives us a metaphor, a powerful, unconscious representation of the issue, with which to work. For instance, the person in our present example might continue, "It's like the world is throwing rocks at me and giving me ice cream in equal measure right now." This is a great way of putting it, and more importantly is how the client's unconscious is framing it to us. It is like having a mirror that shows the hidden face of the situation (which is itself a metaphor!). Once we have this metaphor, we can use it to create a spread, as we did in the previous chapter.

Rocks and Ice Cream Spread

Whilst you may never use this spread, as it was designed for one person on the basis of their unique metaphor, you can perform it by simply laying out six cards in the order given in the diagram and read them as follows:

Rocks and Ice Cream Spread

1. What is the most dangerous problem or issue facing the querent (or myself) now?
2. What is the most dangerous temptation (to be avoided) facing the querent (or myself) now?
3. How can the querent or myself use the challenges and turn them into advantages?
4. In what way can the querent or myself enjoy the situation?
5. What lesson is being taught long-term from the situation?
6. What could go wrong if the querent or myself have too many good things happening?

Just imagine, too, if every reading you design a bespoke spread that you never use again, making every reading face-to-face a totally unique experience for that person and yourself.

Asking the Question Out Loud—Yes or No?

Whilst some readers have told us they do not need to actually hear the client's question, they are somewhat stuck when we ask them how they know that they are not performing a reading for a question that is against their own ethics, e.g., "Should my four-year-old brother stop taking his medication?" You can see why clarification in such a case would be useful, and you may make a policy choice that you want to always have the question stated.

You can also tell the client that even if you do not know the question before starting, the reading will probably home in on it anyway. Some clients wish to withhold the question because they are testing the reader, which is a game that should not be encouraged. If the reading is indeed a game from the client's point of view, it should be stated so, which gives the reader the opportunity to play or refuse the game.

In some cases, the question is so personal or difficult to articulate that it is reasonable not to force clients to reveal it when they have stated that they do not wish to. These cases should be taken on an individual basis, and in our experience it is usually apparent when it is not a control issue or a game. These are often the readings that provide the most memorable and life-affecting results.

Rephrasing the Question

This issue continues the theme of control, empowerment, and the relationship between yourself and the client. When a person gives you a question, do you feel as if you might wish to rephrase it? Many readers discuss this issue, and there is no real hard-and-fast answer. You might wish to consider that in rephrasing a question, you may be implying that the client does not know the "right" question, dependent on how you go about it. On the other hand, rephrasing the question assures that you understand it.

If you are going to rephrase the question, do it in partnership with the other person, keeping the emphasis on comprehension and clarification. We have heard readers on a range of tarot podcasts, online readings, TV psychic shows, and other venues simply "override" the questioner in favour of their preferred restatement of the question, like so: "So, Gary, you've asked about whether your boss has it in for you, and I am going to ask the cards, 'Where should Gary look for a better job since his boss is a schmuck?'" This is obviously not appropriate on a number of different levels.

When and How to Say No

Many readers tell us they have difficulties saying no to a question. One reader we know actually charges by the interest level of the question—ask a boring (to him) question and he charges a lot, but if you present him a more unusual or fascinating (to him) one, he might even do the reading for free. That's a fairly unique filter to apply to questions, but it ensures he faces only readings in which he has a financial and personal interest.

The general rule, of course, is that you can say no to any question you are asked and do not necessarily have to give any reason beyond "I have chosen not to read for this question at this time," or perhaps "I am afraid for professional (or personal) reasons I cannot perform this reading for you." The way you decline will depend upon the circumstance; however, keeping it short, polite, and professional is the best guide, and not getting drawn into further discussion is essential. There is no need to apologise for not performing a reading.

Handling an Intense Question

Often a reader will face an emotionally difficult or intense question. As this can come out of the blue, there is no firm rule for dealing with it, other than to be prepared for anything. We suggest that you always have tissues to hand in a face to face environment, although not situated directly on the table in front of the clients as if you expect them to cry! In the case of a situation that is obviously overwhelming the client, you might consider referring him or her to an appropriate support network. In the UK, our telephone directory contains two useful pages with contact details of every support network imaginable, and we have this torn out and in our journal so it is on hand for readings. Most US directories have something similar.

Sometimes an answer can be intense from the cards themselves—intense for you or for the other person, or sometimes for you both. That is why every reading should be considered as having the potential to go somewhere deep, even if the setting may not be appropriate for such diving. If a reading starts to become intense at a setting such as a birthday party, you can always say that you will record the cards on your notepad—you do have a notepad ready, don't you?—and will return to it with the client the following day or in a more suitable environment. If they agree, then this is a good way of properly and appropriately handling the situation. For this reason, it is always preferable to have as much privacy as possible for your readings, regardless of the venue.

Dealing with a Repeat Question

Sometimes a client will return to ask the same question again, and sometimes they will return a third time, or a fourth, or a fifth … you get the idea. We believe that this is not a particularly useful, ethical, or practical situation for either party. At a recent conference/workshop with Rachel Pollack and Mary K. Greer, it was generally agreed that this is a common situation that needs to be dealt with immediately when it arises.

In a sense, this is similar to the "saying no" section above, and requires that you define clear boundaries from the outset. It is generally the case (and there are always exceptions, of course) that a reading will cover a future period of about three months, or perhaps even a year ahead. Many times, the reading will require a few months' processing by the client in the present as a means of self-discovery. Some readers adopt a three-meeting model, with clearly defined gaps between sessions, when working with tarot as a self-discovery tool. Setting clear boundaries at the outset and then sticking with them is the most important part of working with others face to face. These boundaries protect all parties and establish clear frameworks in which the reading can actually be the focus of attention.

Handling Questions of Payment

Questions of payment usually arise during the initial meeting with the client. A clear definition should be made at the outset and you should not offer this as an apologetic or personal delivery; any transaction is a trade and covered by laws and regulations. It is highly unlikely anyone will take you to court (see www.fortunetellinglaws.com) unless you are acting fraudulently; however, you should be absolutely clear up front about the amount expected and the duration of the reading, as well as your policies on refunds and recourse.

It's All in the Question

In this section, we will share details of our survey of more than eighty thousand questions presented to tarot readers, to help you be entirely confident, prepared, and fearless, no matter what you get asked by a querent. A handful of major themes run through the list: love and heartbreak, soul mates and reincarnation, spiritual growth, money and work, children, and health. All of these themes affect each other; they are not separate but part of one big whole.

As we look at these questions, first and foremost we must always remember to tread lightly. As with any work that involves deep dialogue with another soul, we are reminded: "Human Fragility—Handle with Care!" We are not in the business of answering questions as if they were examinations to get correct; we are explorers in the deepest of oceans and the darkest of skies.

Love and Relationships

A high percentage of questions asked are in relation to love, longing, and heartbreak. In fact, three out of every five questions you will be asked will be in this category.[14] Here are some typical examples.

I really don't want to make a choice; I'm a Sagittarian. Can I keep two relationships going on at the same time?

I am finding it hard to keep my faith about meeting a future partner; I have been waiting all my life and still I have to go it alone. What do I have to do to feel better about myself and being alone?

How can I find the man of my dreams who wishes to settle down with me? What do I have to do to find everlasting happiness in a relationship?

To break down this first question, we can focus on "choice" and "two relationships." A little knowledge of astrology here would be useful, along with its correspondences to the tarot cards. We would be aware that a Gemini, Sagittarius's opposite sign, would be more amenable to a split in this situation, but a Sagittarian would be keen to keep the momentum going. The major arcana card Temperance, which corresponds to Sagittarius, embodies the energies that may be needed for our querent to gain some clarity from the reading. This could be described as a "guidance" card to throw light on the situation. We could choose it as a significator and place it in the centre of the reading, and then use a standard spread such as the Celtic Cross.

In the second question, there is obviously a conflict. The person wants to have faith in the future; however he also wants to know what to do if that faith is not answered in reality. In this case, we may want to answer the question about living alone, or else gently enquire if they want to rephrase the first part of what they have presented as their actual question. It is more difficult to read when we have a "schizophrenic" or paradoxical question like this one, and far better to call these to clarification before we start the reading.

Our third example carries us onto our next theme, soul mates, which often overlaps questions about love and romance. There are two parts of the question, which we would break down into "how do I live my life now to attract the right person for me?" and "what do I need to know to build a healthy relationship?"

We would perhaps lay out three to five cards for the first part of the question, and the same number for the second part of the question. We can then read the two lines as answers to the two questions, and also compare the two lines, showing how the questions are connected.

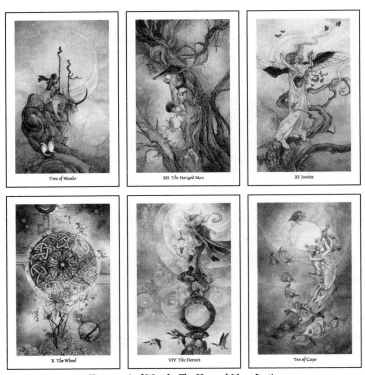

Top row: 2 of Wands, The Hanged Man, Justice
Bottom row: The Wheel of Fortune, The Hermit, 10 of Cups (Shadowscapes Tarot)

A Spread For Attraction and Building Relationships

In the first line, we read that to attract the right person, our querent needs to "survey the scene" (2 of Wands) by perhaps looking over new interests and hobbies that they may never have expected (The Hanged Man). Whatever may be unexpected, the opposite of their usual activity. The Zumba practitioner should look at meditation classes, the yoga student should get out there to a stock-car rally. This will lead to "Justice" being served and the more the difference, the more attractive the person will become.

In the second line, to then maintain the long-term relationship, we see that the querent must learn to think long-term, taking into considerations ups and downs (The Wheel of Fortune). They should not get off the wheel on its first revolution! They may need to consider taking time out over the course of building the relationship (The Hermit) and this will result in the Ten of Cups, the "Happy Ever After" card! What a positive reading.

We can then compare the pairs, to see how the first part of the question builds into the other. We compare the Two of Wands with the Wheel of Fortune, seeing that by taking a wider viewpoint, trying new horizons, we get stretched to understand life is a cycle of ups and downs. The more we look out, and the further we look, the more we learn to ride the cycle. In the second pair, we see the Hanged Man and the Hermit— both cards of solitary "hanging out." It signifies that by connecting to our own inner values and accepting different parts of ourself, introspection, we become more of ourselves and prove a shining light to others. Finally, in the third pair, Justice leading to the Ten of Cups, we immediately see that what we put into life is rewarded equally—the scales respond to what we put into them.

Another common question is of the form, "When will Dwayne come back to me?" in which we always prefer to work with the querent to resolve into the far more useful, "What can I do for myself whilst others sort out their own life?" A good "Waiting for Dwayne" spread is our Boomerang Spread.

Catching (or Avoiding) the Boomerang Spread

This spread addresses a re-phrasing of the "When will Dwayne (or Dwaynetta) come back to me?" question into "How do I live to my best in the current situation with Dwayne?" It uses a sense of humour with which the querent readily identifies to give serious information in a light-hearted way, by using the recognisable metaphor of a boomerang, allied with some terms from the sport.

Imagine the other person is a boomerang that is presently released from you. Shuffle and lay out six cards in a crescent, like a boomerang. Read them as follows.

1. The Aussie Round position—this card shows how you can return to your centre having released the boomerang.
2. Long Distance position—this card shows the nature of the relationship between you and your Dwayne.
3. Endurance position—this card illustrates how to best endure the to-ing and fro-ing of the relationship for your long-term emotional well-being.
4. Juggling position—the card here weighs up whether to let the boomerang go or try and retrieve it.
5. Consecutive Catch—this card depicts how to learn for all relationships, whether this one or a future one.
6. Trick Catch—this card gives an unusual solution to the present nature of the relationship.

Here is an example of this reading, which demonstrates how profound information can be delivered in the guise of an Australian tradition.

Left to right: 5 of Pentacles, The Hierophant,
Knight of Cups, 6 of Swords, King of Swords, 10 of Swords
(Shadowscapes Tarot)

Here we see that to return to one's centre, one needs to make a "connection" in difficult times. As Barbara Moore writes in the companion booklet to the Shadowscapes deck, for the 5 of Pentacles, "salvation is not far off, if you can make that connection and see past the mental and physical blockades. Even the thorny bush that she views as her only companion bears flowers."

The relationship card, the Hierophant, shows a power struggle in the relationship, with our Dwayne believing themselves to be the teacher, and perhaps indeed they have a lesson for our querent.

The Knight of Cups shows that to endure the relationship, we must advise the querent to be one who "follows his dreams." This is a card of following one's own vision, engaging in one's own quest—Dwayne was merely a station on the way, it appears.

To weigh up the relationship, we turn to the 6 of Swords, indicating again that movement is required, that we must carry ourselves and our own burdens away from the present situation. This is also an opportunity to travel.

The Knight of Swords continues and develops this theme—almost Arthurian in nature—that in future, we must be more discerning in our relationships, lay out the groundrules clearly, and wield our own power.

And finally, the 10 of Swords, our "trick catch" gives a fascinating insight into a potential solution—to really capture the "spiralling and uncontrolled plunge" and ride it out. To almost revel in the distress and really make the most of it—lots of comfort eating and crying, late-night calls to friends—this will perhaps serve to get it resolved far faster than trying to ignore it or "deal with it."

Now we will look at what happens with regard to soul-mates on our tarot table.

Soul Mates and Reincarnation

What is a soul mate, and do we all have one? Do we meet that special one in many lifetimes, over and over again? Having a greater understanding of the concepts involved will assist you when you are faced with these questions.

It has been said that human beings are on a quest to reunite with that which we once were—a fully self-sufficient "love" centre, equipped to be at the centre of our own attention. Plato wrote in the *Symposium* that human nature was "originally one and we were a whole, and the desire and pursuit of the whole is called love." So it is programmed in our nature to seek out love, over and over again, to attain the state of being "one" again, to fulfill our hunger for "me" love, a love that cannot be taken away or lost, as it belongs entirely to oneself.

Let's take a look at the following question regarding a desire to reconnect with a soul mate:

Recently I have felt a sense of regret for distancing myself from someone I cared for and who cared for me. I have not seen him nor do I know how to contact him, but I still feel a strange connection with him that has not permitted me to move on completely. Did I lose my soul mate?

The keywords here to understanding the phrasing of the question are recently, regret, distancing, cared for, strange connection, and the sense of not being able to move on completely. The biggest concern of the querent is actually, "Did I lose my soul mate?" If we evaluate this in the context of Plato's explanation of soul mates, we see that the querent has a longing for her self to be connected again with the focus of her attention—which, as a person, has now moved on. In the present, she herself is left unable to move on.

In our spread for this person, we might look to address the following issues:

· What did the soul mate mean to the querent?
· What part of her "me" did he fulfill? How can she fulfill this role for herself?
· What lessons were learnt?

Here is a more detailed example of a soul-mate connection question, along with a reading for it. Like many relationship questions, it includes an element that the client is probably attempting not to face. What do you make of the likely actual situation that the cards and this interpretation are addressing?

My partner and I live two thousand miles apart, but we share the feeling that we belong together and being together is like home, so we feel we are soul mates. What steps must be taken to allow us to begin sharing our life together, and what is the time frame in which it will happen?

For this reading, we will use the Tarot of the New Vision, which offers a reversed viewpoint from the standard Rider-Waite-Smith deck, and hence a potentially new perspective. It is a useful deck for approaching difficult, stalemated, or apparently irresolvable situations. We'll use a simple seven-card relationship spread. Its positions are: My Partner, Myself, The Connection, Common Base, Resources of the Partner, Resources of the Querent, and Focal Point. The question, in essence, is "How and when will this relationship develop?"

Card 1. My Partner: Eight of Pentacles

Here we see a character who is working to build a business. However, not all is as it seems: his expensive-looking shirt is merely a play-actor's shirt, worn to give the appearance of success without it actually being present. Another figure is creating a statue of a rich merchant holding a money bag. This signifies that the partner is likely interested in the outer trappings of wealth and material stability, but may not have all the resources to create and maintain such stability without assistance. In a relationship reading, this may serve to remind the querent that she may be seen as a partner on a superficial, financial level rather than an emotional one.

Card 2. Myself (the Querent): Seven of Pentacles

This card continues the theme of the first card, and offers a picture of a figure looking down at a plant upon which he has toiled. In a regular deck, this signifies disappointment, since the investment (here, emotional) has not produced the crop (relationship) that was expected. There is an air of futility. In the New Vision deck, this card further adds a female ghostly spirit looking down on the figure, as if to say, "I could have helped you but it is too late now." In a sense, this card suggests that it is now too late to undo the past, so a new start must be made.

Card 3. The Connection: Ace of Wands

The connecting card is a powerful indicator of shared values, ambitions, goals, and a shared lifestyle. What connects the partners in this relationship is not purely emotional sharing but a shared vision of how life should be lived. This connection is what holds the relationship together, so if it has changed on either side, the relationship will suffer accordingly. It tells us to ensure that we have decided on our own values and what we will accept in our life, and that we have clearly communicated those same values to our partner.

Card 4. Common Base: Temperance

This major arcana card represents not just "temperance" as in patience and harmony, but also "tempering" as in the method of making a steel sword. The metal is heated and then rapidly quenched, then reheated and quenched, over and over, until it is very sharp but also very brittle. It appears that the partners' common base in this relationship is this alchemy of on/off and hot/cold and the resulting tension. If the situation changes and that tension is missing, the relationship will feel baseless and unfounded. It is up to the partners whether they work to change the base of the relationship or continue in this way.

Card 5. Resources of the Partner: The Empress

This second of the three major arcana cards in this reading is the Empress, a card of motherhood, fertility, pregnancy, and growth. It is perhaps unusually in the position of the male partner here. It may signify that the partner's relationship with his own mother and upbringing is now bearing heavily on the love relationship—a situation that may call for deep understanding, communication, and even counselling. It may also symbolise the partner's need for security that he brings into the love relationship. It further shows that the partner has emotional depth that can be tapped into.

Card 6. Resources of the Querent: King of Wands

Again, it is somewhat unusual that the masculine King of Wands is in the female position of the reading, just as the feminine Empress was in the male position. The King of Wands is someone who knows his own mind and can hold strongly to his core values, gained through experience. It signifies, with regard to the Ace of Wands, that the querent has been holding the relationship together more than the partner. The saving grace of the King of Wands is his honesty and straightforwardness. The querent should take the opportunity to be as forthright and honest as possible. This is her best resource to develop the relationship.

Card 7. Focal Point: Justice

The focal point for the relationship is the major arcana card Justice. This signifies that the relationship has come to a head when everything of the past is being weighed up. The scales must contain everything, both past and recent events, in order to judge the situation correctly. This requires communication and openness from both parties.

It seems in this reading that the relationship is certainly at a tipping point, and that the former hot/cold energy has turned into a stalemate where little is communicated. As this is so unlike the tension that actually holds the relationship together, it will no doubt feel as if there is a total void of emotion. The only way forward is for everything to be weighed up impartially, with a cold eye.

The transposition of the strong male/female energies in the two partnership cards is very striking. One wonders how that has played out in the relationship and what changed it in the past to lead to the current situation. The reading as a whole is not entirely hopeless, but it is troubled. There are a number of cards within it that indicate stress; the financial situation may not be as it appears, and this is one of the things that needs to be cleared up for "justice" to be reached within the relationship.

Spiritual Growth

It will come as no surprise that a large proportion of the questions asked of a tarot reader are of a spiritual nature, with emphasis on one's spiritual path and development. The very fact that the querent is consulting a tarot reader implies that he or she is more aware than most of the importance of that which is not physically tangible.

Here are three such questions:

- What do I need to know in order to improve my spiritual life?
- The improvement of spiritual life is a matter of depth and one in which the tarot can help provide guidance and illumination. There are many aspects of the study of tarot that take a philosophical, religious, or spiritual approach to our experience of life. One simple answer to the question is to provide a deck of tarot cards for the querent themselves and teach them how to use it. We will also provide a spread to approach this question.
- I feel disconnected from my path, afraid and uncertain. What am I doing with my life?
- A total disconnection with one's life can often come about from a re-organisation of one's values, the bedrock of our human experience. In a positive way, this functions much as a gear system on a vehicle, where the clutch plate pulls away from the crankshaft in order to reduce friction when the gear is changed. In much the same way, this disconnection in life can function to provide a space for introspection and re-gearing of values. The tarot—along with journaling—has proven a remarkable tool for carrying out this inner re-organisation for many people.
- I have started on a new course to learn about paganism, which I feel may be calling to me. How should I make the most of this course, and is there anything specific I should do?
- Again, with these types of questions, there is often a tarot deck to deal with the specifics. In this case, we have a range of pagan-based decks to hand to answer the question, from the Druidcraft

for pagans to the Necronomicon for those deciding to follow a Lovecraftian path—the whole spectrum is covered. One can often learn more about new approaches such as paganism by acquiring a reputable deck from within that system and making use of it. The following spread also can be utilised with different "spiritual system" decks.

The Spiritual Pyramid Spread

Shuffle and lay out ten cards in a pyramid.

1

2 3

4 5 6

7 8 9 10

The cards are read as follows and relate to the four levels of Kabbalah, or four worlds:

- 1: What is the spiritual core that informs me at this time? What am I being called to aspire to?
- 2 + 3: What must I create in my life?
- 4 + 5 + 6: What resources is the spiritual universe providing for me to accomplish the above?
- 7 + 8 + 9 + 10: What elements of my life must be drawn together to manifest my spiritual life? These four cards can also be read in detail as the four tools of the elements in matter, so the first card relates to "Lifestyle," the second to "Creativity," the third to "Education & Learning," and the fourth to the "Physical and Material Resources."

Here is an example of how this spiritual pyramid can provide a full overview in answer to one of the questions above, in this case, "I have started on a new course to learn about paganism, which I feel may be calling to me. How should I make the most of this course, and is there anything specific I should do?"

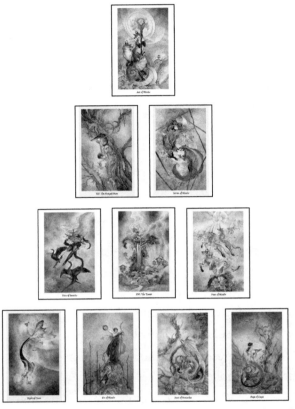

Top to bottom, left to right: Ace of Wands, The Hanged Man, 7 of Wands, 5 of Swords, The Tower, 4 of Wands, 8 of Cups, 6 of Wands, 4 of Pentacles, Page of Cups (Shadowscapes Tarot)

Here we have a powerful spiritual card, the very root of spirit, in the uppermost position, showing the person is experiencing a powerful spiritual calling in their discovery of paganism. The Foxes in this particular deck show how they encourage intellect and wit, meaning that the seekers mind will be engaged enthusiastically in their discoveries.

In terms of creating in life, the Hanged Man and the 7 of Wands shows that the seeker will be able to bring into their path a whole new perspective and new insights, perhaps upturning old values.

The resources that can be drawn upon, with that Tower in the middle of the row, are all about clearing the ground for new things. The seeker will bring new thoughts into their field, quite rapidly, and not have time for outworn traditions.

Finally, taking each card in the bottom row separately, we see that the mundane life can be arranged to the spiritual concerns:

- Lifestyle: 8 of Cups—Allowing oneself the luxury of immersing oneself deeply in the path, using dreams and visions to engage with the pagan ideal. Abandonment to the emotional enjoyment of trance, dance and pleasure within the path.
- Creativity: 6 of Wands—Finding a good balance between making your voice heard and listening to others, particularly the "in crowd" who are already within the tradition.
- Education: 4 of Pentacles—Not extending too much into buying education, books, or resources. Not getting carried away into the "spiritual supermarket shopping" syndrome.
- Physical and Material Resources: Page of Cups—Using your creativity to provide resources. The Seeker may have some artistic gift to offer the pagan community in return for material reward.

Money and Work

Money—how to make it, win it, save it, or invest it—is a never-ending topic in the world of divining. So how do you go about doing a reading in a fresh way, as if it is the first time these questions have ever been posed? And with regard to ethical considerations, how and when do you recommend the client should get more specialised guidance such as financial advice, legal advice, career advice, or just plain old parental advice?

We think it's important to remember that your only role is as a tarot reader, so try to stick to reading the cards. You will not go far wrong with old-fashioned common sense and a fair dose of compassion thrown in. Since you're probably not a financial expert (unless, of course, that is what you do in your full-time job), please stick to what you know best and listen to what the cards have to say.

I am single and self-employed, and the company that rented me working space has just closed down. Should I spend money in extending my home or look for an alternative space to rent? I currently have no income.

This would be a tricky question to even ask an MBA-educated consultant. Although, having said that, if one had no money, it is unlikely that one could even afford to ask such a consultant. Here we must avoid being tempted to give direct advice from our own sense of entrepreneurship and simply read the cards.

I have invested money into the business where I work; however, I feel like some dishonesty is going on. I would like to ask if there is anything I should be aware of, or should I prepare for something like losing my job?

Again, business ethics and practice are not our field of expertise, so we should perhaps look at rephrasing the question, or certainly concentrate on where the tarot may assist—preparing for the unforeseen, the latter part of the question. The question also appears to demonstrate a lack of communication at work, another area where the tarot can provide insight. It can also give another source of information to the querent and respond to the insecurity in the question.

I want to work as an art therapist and further my sculpting career. How can I make this possible and be able to live comfortably off it, so that I can quit my current job by September of this year?

Here we have a specific timing issue, and an otherwise straightforward inquiry to our oracle, where a person wishes to make a significant change in their life. Again, we must be careful not to drift into our own viewpoints, even if we have had a similar experience. Always return to what the cards are saying in dialogue, and if you have commentary to add from your own life, make this absolutely clear. A good reader has a wide perspective and experience, and can bring that to the table in a face-to-face encounter.

Sometimes a simple one-card draw can be a means of answering a question and sticking to the point. Here we pull a single card for the investment and honest question above, and receive the 10 of Pentacles. If we also want to remove bias, it is a good method to simply read from the book! Take one of your tarot books, or the companion guide to the deck, and simply read it aloud. Even for long-experienced professionals, there are good opportunities to go back to the book. In this case, we read for the 10 of Pentacles, "enjoying affluence, desiring the permanence that financial security can bring, and being able to appreciate the luxury and the good fortune that has befallen you. This is the ultimate in worldly success, the result of long-term efforts finally brought to fruition, of finally being able to settle into a lasting beneficial situation and position" (Shadowscapes, pp. 231-2). This was an entirely random draw for that real question, and shows that the insecurity is perhaps unwarranted. When you trust yourself to read straight from a book, it can have a massive effect on the querent, as you remove yourself from the dialogue completely—do not be afraid to try it on occasion.

Great Expectations

What do I need to know about conceiving a child over the next year?

Unless you are a trained gynecological, medical professional and the client is under your care in that capacity, it is sensible to approach questions of this nature very carefully—firstly by stressing that you are not in a position to read for a question phrased like the one above. However, the question can be rephrased or reframed to focus on a more general theme of creativity, nurturing, and productivity.

The first part of the querent's question is primarily about the "I." This is the first clue about how to approach the cards with this query. What does the "I" need to know about her sense of self? Ask the cards what she needs to learn and discover about herself over the next year, which may be what she really needs to know. Conception might well be part of that overall discovery.

Other questions can include:

- *What do I need to know about conceiving a baby?*
- *Will my baby be healthy?*
- *Is my baby to be a boy or girl?*
- *Should I continue with the IVF treatment?*

Again, the same rule applies to each of these—we are not medical consultants. We can cast a reading for the general energies and influences at play, and interpret those for the most likely outcome and advice given that reading of the cards. It is up to the querent to add this reading into their total pool of information. On some occasions, though, the reading can be very dramatic. We did one reading using the Psycards, an oracle deck with simple and no-nonsense cards, for a pregnancy question, and the three cards which came up were YES, BIRTH, and THE SAGE (which is read as the Doctor or Teacher). This hardly required any interpretation at all.

Health and Well-being

Tali's mother once told her that one day she would realise that the most important things in her life would be her health and the health of those nearest and dearest to her. At the time, she was only fifteen years old, so the realities of sickness, aches and pains, and loss had not yet come home to roost. We become aware of such things at a later stage in our life.

It is an interesting statistic that the average age of a tarot reader is forty-four years old.[15] This has a direct influence on the questions asked by the average querent, since the querent audience tends to reflect the makeup of the readers providing the service. It is a little like the audience of a pop concert reflecting the age and the values of the performers on stage. Tarot readers will find themselves being asked over and over again questions relating to health and well-being. This of course touches upon questions of relationships and finances, among other concerns, because there is no such thing as a two-dimensional question in tarot. We have found that the question evolves even as it is being asked. Here are some examples:

- *My partner has been quite ill and I just got laid off from my job. We're both under a lot of stress and I don't know if our relationship will survive.*
- *I suffer from a debilitating medical condition. What can I do to improve my quality of life?*
- *I've tried everything to lose weight and just can't. Why am I stuck at this weight?*
- *Will my wife survive her illness or will she die?*

As we can see from these questions, health issues are the most serious we may face in our tarot encounters, as well as our own personal lives. The use of tarot in these circumstances should be carried out with respect and sensitivity. We should look to use spreads or methods that provide new insight and connection to the larger patterns of life, empowering (for want of a better word) the querent to the best standard of life and connection during the time of illness—in themselves or others. A simple health spread is as follows.

The Dis-ease Spread

1. In what manner has this issue come about?
2. What can I do to support all the other care and attention being placed upon me?
3. How am I separate from the condition?
4. How am I connected to the condition?
5. What role does this condition play in my life?
6. How can I best consider the condition?

Here is a real reading from a querent with a colostomy, one which they have had for a while and wished to consider having long-term insight into the condition.

Left to right: 3 of Wands, Page of Pentacles, 9 of Wands,
10 of Wands, 3 of Swords, 2 of Swords (Shadowscapes Tarot)

Here we see that the arising issue may have come about from the fiery energy of the wands leading the system astray, without control—the 3 of Wands sets things in motion but does not monitor them. It represents an impetus that has remained unchecked, leading to the issue that required the surgery.

The Page of Pentacles shows that the querent can take little steps to benefit from the care and attention placed upon them, concentrating on practical daily issues. It also shows they should build up their material well-being by working, in a small way.

The next two cards we look at together, seeing that the person is separate from their colostomy in the sense of it is all complete now (the "nine" in the stages one to ten) and has been overcome. They are connected to it in the sense of carrying the condition and managing it—leading to new values.

The role the condition plays is in providing a transformation and separateness in which that transformation can take place—the 3 of Swords. The best consideration of the situation is provided by the 2 of Swords, keeping all things in balance.

Facing the Absurd

At one time or another, we will all encounter a question that makes us want to laugh or presses our raised-eyebrow button. However, we are (hopefully) good-mannered individuals who have suppressed our chuckles in the most delicate of occasions. So how would you handle the following unusual questions?

An item from my prized collection of stuffed owls has been stolen. How can I find it? Shall I contact a medium, a dowsing specialist, or a remote viewer? I thought I would come to a tarot reader first.

How do I decide between learning Jedi mind tricks and learning tarot reading as a way of giving back to my community, without giving up my Star Trek fan fiction writing, editing, and publishing?

I have been told by a trusted psychic that I will get engaged to a man named Dwayne—people call him Dee for short—and she also said that he is a fire sign or linked to fire in some way. Can you please tell me if this is true and maybe tell me a little more about him, like where he lives, what his job is, and where I'll meet him?

Have I any connection to King Henry VIII, as I feel I have a connection? Also, how can I improve my fifteen-year-old marriage?

Of course, in all of these cases—and many more you will encounter for yourself—we should honour the question and respond appropriately. Our role is to read the cards while recognizing our own responses. We should not be unprepared for questions that may well be totally outside of our box. One of the joys of tarot face to face is that our own box is constantly being expanded to comprehend the diversity of life. Furthermore, a legitimate concern often lurks beneath the most seemingly ludicrous questions. Use creative questioning, as we discussed earlier, to try and discover the "real" issues.

Spreads for Hope, Assistance, and Possibilities

Often a question is framed in the most hopeless of terms. The participant feels totally helpless, powerless, and rudderless, or cannot find any sense of confidence. They have come to us as the oracle at the very edge of their despair. In the following methods, we ensure that we acknowledge these powerful feelings, incorporate them, and use tarot to respond in the most useful manner. We do not try to sugarcoat our readings, or offer bland affirmation and empowerment; we face the problem head-on and try to help the client deal with it. Whenever possible, we also take the problem as an opportunity for spiritual learning, raising our perception beyond the situation.

The Finding Possibilities Method

In some cases, we will be asked to read the cards for a situation that seems to have no possibilities at all. The event or situation as framed and presented by the client is so hopeless, stuck, out of control, or complex that no single question will address it. Luckily, we do indeed have a full deck of possibilities and our cards will readily comprehend such situations.

The Star
(Mystic Dreamer Tarot)

Faced with this type of reading, we do not reframe the situation or try to force it into a question. We simply select the major arcana card that illustrates the situation most closely and divine further information by using it as a significator. If the participant feels hopeless, we acknowledge this and suggest that out of all the cards in the deck, there is one that is the card of hope—the Star. This method also works with a range of situations where something is seen as missing or impossible to regain.

We can begin by talking about how the Star represents both hope and vision—a vision likely clouded over because the querent feels so hopeless. It is also a card of the future, and so is relevant too when there is no future seen in the present circumstances.

We then ask the participant to look at the card for a moment, dwell upon it, and then return it into the deck. We might tell him that every moment in his life is connected to this point of divination, and that every moment in his future is likewise connected.

Ask him to shuffle the deck whilst really considering his hopeless situation. He must truly connect to the feelings of his circumstances and look at them face to face.

When he is satisfied that he has connected to the issue and finished shuffling, take the deck and turn it face-up.

Say, "We will now find hope and the possibilities it offers." Search through the deck, in order, until you find the Star again. You can then read and interpret the two cards on either side of it to identify the possibilities for regaining hope. They have been attracted to the Star to show the possibilities in even the most hopeless situation.

As an advanced method, you can read the four or eight cards on either side of the Star card, taking the ones below it as the past and the ones above it as the future of the situation. This will create a linear, eight- or sixteen-card reading.[16] You can also use this as a second method following a more detailed reading, or in advance of a more specific reading, as often a specific question may arise or become obvious once this method has been applied.

So if you had a situation where the person feels that he has lost all confidence, you would repeat this method with the Emperor card, or if he felt unloved, the Lovers card, and so forth. You would say in the first case, "Let us now find power, and the possibilities it offers," and in the latter case, "We will now find love, and the possibilities it offers." We give here a table of the major cards and their relation to certain situations; you are encouraged to consider your own associations, too.

Card	Situation	Example statement from querent
0: The Fool	Loss of freedom, possibilities.	"I'm stuck at work, and they seem to have taken all chance of promotion from me. I'm terrified I'm going to be trapped there forever. What do the cards say?"
1: The Magician	Missing the big picture, not having all the facts, being tricked.	"There's something going on with my family that I just can't see. What is it?"
2: The High Priestess	Loss of wonder and mystery, feeling disconnected.	"Since the divorce, I've felt like all the magic has gone from my life. How can I get back my trust?"
3: The Empress	Stagnant situation, not getting what you deserve.	"I give and give, but get nothing back. What can I do?"
4: The Emperor	Powerlessness or feeling out of control. Issues of dominance with no escape.	"Whilst all of this is going on, I can't do anything about it. I feel helpless and my confidence is all gone."
5: The Hierophant	Being stuck in the rules or the system.	"My family seems to think it's okay for this event to happen, but I am not so sure."
6: The Lovers	Having no choice.	"There's a chance to retire or a transfer; however, neither is what I want."

7: The Chariot	Not being able to move forward in any way.	"Until I sell my house, I cannot do anything, but there's no movement in the market. What will happen?"
8: Strength	Being unbalanced; not being able to find a place of peace.	"My course is proving more stressful than I thought and I cannot find time to study at home, either."
9: The Hermit	Feeling totally alone.	"Nobody knows what I am going through, and I cannot get advice at all. What can I do?"
10: The Wheel of Fortune	Feeling that luck has turned completely against you.	"It's been one thing after another, and I'm dreading what might be next."
11: Justice	When the law has been taken out of your hands.	"The social services are taking over what is going on, and whilst I am really happy about that, I wonder what will become of me?"
12: The Hanged Man	When a situation is moving between two extremes.	"I just swing between being content and bored, with no in-between."
13: Death	When a situation should be changing but shows no sign of doing so.	"Why hasn't it happened yet?"
14: Temperance	The environment is out of control and negativity is spilling everywhere.	"There was a whisper campaign behind my back and now even my friends seem to be turning against me."

15: The Devil	You are in a dark place inside.	"Since the divorce, I have just felt really bad about myself."
16: The Tower	Some event has shocked you into immobility.	"Of course, it was so sudden that I'm not sure that I'll ever be able to move on."
17: The Star	There is no hope.	"It's truly a hopeless situation, isn't it?"
18: The Moon	You cannot see any path ahead, which is frightening.	"So I have to move, which is terrifying, or I could go back to my parents, which is even worse."
19: The Sun	People do not seem to be aware of the problem.	"I keep telling my friends and work colleagues, but no one seems to see it the way I do."
20: Judgement	You feel you have lost your calling or your direction.	"It's like being a yacht bobbing on the ocean without any sails."
21: The World	There are no resources or reinforcements on which to call; all your energy has gone.	"I'm too tired to do anything about it and it is getting worse."

The Kabbalah Path Method

Like those who feel hopeless, many querents come for a reading when they feel stuck or like they've "hit a brick wall" and can see no future progress. This is a limiting belief because the world is constantly undergoing change, and no situation can remain the same, no matter what we think of it. In this method, we use the Jewish mystical system of Kabbalah, particularly the Tree of Life diagram on which the tarot can be placed, to resolve a stuck situation. It uses the Kabbalistic associations reflected in the tarot to identify the question and its answer.

You do not need to know anything about Kabbalah to perform this method, although the more you learn about other esoteric systems, the more layers you can add to your readings.

Split your deck into two piles, the first containing only the majors and the second containing both the minors and the court cards.

Ask the participant to shuffle the majors while considering her stuck situation. Ask her to select one card and lay it down, face-up.

This card, through arcane Kabbalistic correspondences, now defines the two positions (Sephiroth) that it connects on the Tree of Life. See the table below for assistance.

Shuffle the deck of minors and court cards and place a card in the first and second positions having been indicated by the major card.

The first card selected should go in the lowest numbered position (higher of the two Sephiroth) above the major card, and the second card selected (lower of the two Sephiroth) should be placed below the major card.

These will give you the key to your issue. This method is perfect for situations where you do not even know the right question to ask.

Major Arcana Card	Connects
The Fool	1–2
The Magician	1–3
The High Priestess	1–6
The Empress	2–3
The Emperor	2–6
The Hierophant	2–4
The Lovers	3–6
The Chariot	3–5
Strength	4–5
The Hermit	4–6
The Wheel of Fortune	4–7

Justice	5–6
The Hanged Man	4–8
Death	6–7
Temperance	6–9
The Devil	6–8
The Tower	7–8
The Star	7–9
The Moon	7–10
The Sun	8–9
Judgement	8–10
The World	9–10

Key to the Two Positions

1. What is the point trying to come through
2. What is trying to be created
3. What is trying to be constructed
4. That which is expanding
5. That which is contracting
6. The beautiful point of harmony here
7. The cycle this is upon
8. The sense it is trying to make heard
9. The way in which it appears
10. What is really going on, deep down

Note that the first/higher card position is more spiritual than the second/lower card position. The latter is the mundane reflection of the former.

An Example Reading

Suppose you have a situation in which you hardly know where to turn after a significant relationship change. You shuffle the twenty-two major cards whilst considering the situation and draw the Hierophant. Place this in the centre of your table.

You consult the table and find that the Hierophant connects positions 2 and 4.

This means that the position above the Hierophant is defined by 2 (what is trying to be created) and below it by 4 (that which is expanding).

You then shuffle the minor and court cards and select one, which you place above the Hierophant to illustrate what is trying to be created. Then you select a second card, which you place below to show that which is expanding.

If, for example, you had drawn the Nine of Cups above the Hierophant, this might lead you to interpret that what is trying to be created is a situation of self-satisfaction and pride. If you drew the Knight of Wands for the position below, this would indicate that which is expanding is a sense of adventure and independence. This would likely mean positive results because of the relationship change, so long as pride was not the issue.

In this chapter, we hope that you have discovered one thing you cannot predict is the question you will be asked. It is wise to have a fall-back method for any question, and to be able to design spreads on the go to provide unique readings for every type of question. In our survey of tens of thousands of questions, whilst we have seen patterns, every question remains individual. In being a face-to-face reader, you will have an unparalleled opportunity to immerse yourself in the fundamental questions of existence, even if they are presented as "When will Dwayne come back to me." Prepare yourself and your cards, and remain open and curious to every querent—grace, inspiration, and accuracy will inevitably follow.

Four

Facing
the Querent

We were recently in an airport waiting lounge when Marcus received an e-mail on his BlackBerry. As a reward for partially funding a tarot documentary, he would be receiving a tarot reading from New York–based poet and tarot reader Enrique Enriquez. The reading arrived and he had time to look at it before we boarded the plane.

The first line of the reading was something akin to, "These are my words, but they are now not my words. Read them out aloud." Since Marcus is reasonably fearless in public spaces, he began to read them out aloud, without knowing what was beyond his scroll button. It soon became obvious and clear that the reading did not apply to him at all, but rather to Tali. And as the lines progressed and Marcus read them out, it was as if Marcus was an oracle for words that were beyond our comprehension.

The hairs on the back of our necks went up, and Marcus was—for once—speechless. Not only did Enrique have no idea as to the circumstances when Marcus would receive his message, nor who else might be present, but he actually stated that all he does is read the images of the cards and everything else is down to the listener.[17]

The moral of this story is that even in the most modern of circumstances, the oracular tradition of tarot is not dead.

———

Our biggest step in reading tarot is reading it face to face with other people. In our previous chapters, we have seen how we can apply the symbols and context of the cards to real-life situations and how we can overcome the initial obstacles we may place in front of ourselves. We've also prepared ourselves for the questions we will be asked as a tarot reader. Now it's time to explore in more depth the nuances of reading for other people, including how you can use tarot to uncover your own unique and distinctive oracular voice.

Different Decks with Different Voices

Tarot is a language composed of symbol and metaphor, which translates to real life. As such, it has diverse dialects and accents that make your reading style unique. Tarot is very much influenced by the diversity of communication, and how an individual tarot reader perceives and verbally expresses the images that are presented to him or her will vary. Not only that, but the deck used will also impact this communication.

There are up to a thousand tarot decks on the market at the time of writing, and the majority of these are lesser-known and published in the Asia-Pacific area. We are living in a time of abundance and choice. There is no better time to be a consumer of tarot, so be merry and feast on the cornucopia of decks available on the market.

We are often asked which is the best deck, or the top five decks, to purchase. This is a difficult question as one deck may suit you as a reader but not somebody else; art has personal, subjective appeal and mysticism is an even more personal path.

Let's start with the standard, must-have staple of tarot decks, commonly called the Rider-Waite deck. The world of tarot has certainly moved on since the early 1980s when Rachel Pollack wrote of the difficulties of obtaining a copy of this deck in her book *78 Degrees of Wisdom*. More accurately called the Rider-Waite-Smith deck, this is probably the best starter choice, since it set the stage for every seventy-eight card deck following it. A number of variations have been published, such as the Illuminated Tarot, which is a recolouring of the original, or the Smith-Waite Tarot Centennial Edition, featuring scans of the first edition deck, a century old. Furthermore, a whole host of "clone" decks incorporate the symbolism and images from this deck into their own original artwork; thus, if you are familiar with the Rider-Waite-Smith deck, you will be instantly familiar with all of its descendents.

The Thoth Tarot, published in 1942, is a deck that hums with power. It is known for its brutal honesty and unique Kabbalistic symbolism. It was conjured up by the infamous magician Aleister Crowley and designed by the artist Lady Frieda Harris using sacred geometry and occult principles. The original companion book, written by Crowley, is dense and poorly organized; however, there are a number of more helpful contemporary books and courses to guide you through the cards.

There are decks themed and tailored for every occasion and interest that will address your love of whim and whimsy, your longing to delve into the mysterious world of the sacred and the wonderful, and your ever-growing transformation in this remarkable existence we call life on earth. Here are a few other seventy-eight card decks that we find notable (and of use to beginners especially):

- The Robin Wood Tarot (featured in Anthony Louis's *Tarot Plain and Simple* book)
- The Druidcraft Tarot (a Druidic/pagan deck)
- The Morgan-Greer Tarot (a friendly Waite-Smith clone)
- The Mythic Tarot (based on Greek myth)
- The Mystic Faerie Tarot (ideal for teenagers or discovering the teenager within oneself)

We also have our preferred "oracle" decks, which do not follow the standard seventy-eight card pattern. We love the Philosopher's Stone Fortune-Telling Deck, featuring stones in various symbolic illustrations, and the PsyCards, which are based on Carl Jung's work and have cards clearly labeled yes, no, and never—very good for down-and-dirty readings where simple answers are required.

Watch Your Language

Now more than ever, modern language is changing. No two individuals use language in exactly the same way, since we are all influenced by factors such as where we live, our age, our background, our nationality, and especially the growth of the Internet, with the world quickly becoming a global village.

Therefore, in addition to regional differences in accent and vocabulary, we will also encounter different styles of communicating a reading that are very much influenced by the teaching style of a particular tarot teacher. How we think and (of course) how we feel comes through in a tarot reading. Some readers have a tarot voice that expresses more humour (when the context is appropriate, of course) when doing a reading; other readers may prefer to remain more serious.

The topic of context brings us to the importance of being sensitive to the personality of the querent and where he or she is at in life. This is something that comes up in many jobs where communication is a focal point. For instance, we have all met a hairdresser who does not know when to stop talking and just cut the hair! Sometimes, in communicating a reading, less can be more. As Umberto Eco said, "The truth is brief, the rest is merely commentary."

Some research suggests that people find tarot troubling because they think it can "affect the mind" in some unspecified manner. This may be based on a general fear of being controlled; people may fear that their free will could be affected by an external force. Thus we have to take care, when we express what we see and feel through the cards, that our word choice and advice are not misinterpreted. For example, be wary of using the phrases "you should" or "you must"—and particularly "the cards tell me you should..."

Even in the case of what appears to us to be a clear-cut decision, it's important to emphasize that the client has a choice to make and always has the final say. A slight change to a simple turn of phrase can make so much difference to how somebody receives the wisdom of the cards that you are sharing. Notice, too, when you deliver a reading, that you may switch "person" or point of view when speaking. You should try to be aware of the impact of "you can see that..." versus "we can see that..." or "I can see that..." Speaking in the first person—"I feel that the cards are telling me..."—is active and direct; it is a more confident and open voice, and less prone to misinterpretation.

Open Yourself to Inspiration

That precise moment in time when the reader and the querent have been brought together to be with the cards is a magical occurrence. It could even be said that every moment of our life has been leading up to this time, when we impart a message, through the cards, that is destined for the querent. This is true no matter what is said, and no matter how meaningful or how silly you may feel the message is—it has to be said.

It could be one word that resonates and gives you an instant rapport with your client, or you may feel you are burbling many words with no recognition of what you are saying at all. It may be that the querent is merely "taking delivery" of the message now, and it will be many weeks, months, or years until the reading finally makes sense to him or her.

Whatever the case, always go with your inspiration. Always try to find some new way of doing a spread or finding an answer for your client. You may discover that what you are doing has already been done somewhere else by someone else; years later you may even read about it in a book. However, it is important to experiment. Tarot reading is a surprisingly new tool in the long tradition of oracles and fortunetelling, so there is plenty of opportunity to make new discoveries and contribute to the emerging tradition.

There is a lot of the concept of the "long game" in tarot reading. All that is needed is to await the divine will to manifest the moment. To everything there is a season, a time for every purpose under heaven (Ecclesiastes 3:1).

Keep It Professional

As a professional tarot reader, it's your job to keep the reading on track. Keep keenly to the querent's issue and the stated question. Try to avoid being drawn into conversations like whether the querent should alter the décor of her dining room. Remember that you are her reader and not her personal friend; you are also not her therapist. Avoid very personal talk, especially when you hear the "too much information!" alarm in your head. This can be more of a problem if you are reading regularly for the same person over time.

It is possible to remain friendly and professional, yet detached, throughout your tarot card session.[18] What you do not want is for querents to become dependent upon you, especially if they are going through a vulnerable time. If not handled sensitively, this could lead to complications, especially if you have to refuse doing further readings for them. It's not unusual for tarot readers to be bombarded with requests for readings from the same querent who will not take no for an answer.

Keep It Real

Do not pretend to be something that you are not; the tarot calls out your authentic voice, face to face. Ground the reading in what you are looking at. When you flounder, always return to the content of the cards in front of you. If you are overwhelmed with detail, sit back and take in the whole picture of the reading. If you cannot see any detail, look more closely at one specific card. Use your skill of pinpointing to identify what's most important in the reading. Incorporate everything that happens. If you say something "wrong," go with it. You may be surprised where the resulting conversation may take you in that moment.

It's also helpful to refer to your daily experience. For instance, if you work in a shop, use your experience dealing with daily tasks, like sorting clothes. All your life's unique and rich experiences contribute to your readings. The most mundane of events can have significant import when used as a clear and accessible story for a deeper message, through the tarot.

Part of "keeping it real" is recognizing when it gets "unreal." During a reading, you may enter into a trancelike state, even lightly. This is a result of your focused attention, your unconscious mind, and the dreamlike bridging of the cards' symbols and metaphors. If you start to feel slightly strange, explore that feeling and follow it. Recognise and embrace your inner state.

First Impressions Last

Think carefully about the impression you want to give, and remember that old adage, "First impressions last." The first time your querent lays eyes on you and your reading environment is a very special moment that cannot be undone or recreated. The first thing the querent will do is to weigh up you and your space. Is this a place that they feel safe and secure in? Do you look like a person they can trust? Think about how you want to market yourself. What sort of reader are you? Are you an intuitive reader with a mystical vibe about you? That's okay; just be aware of the effect you have on others. There is no getting away from the fact that you are your own walking and talking advertisement.

Props and Regalia

Whilst there are many ways of laying out a table or a space for tarot, the ideal reading area should above all remain functional. There is little worse than a table crammed with crystals, candles, and statues that leave no room to properly lay out the cards.

Of course, many readers like to include favourite objects that give them a sense of connection to the divine, or personal items such as a photo. However, do not forget that these items will also be facing the client, so take into account their impact. You do not want to give a reading that consists of the other person wondering why you have a skull on the table, rather than concentrating on the reading itself.

We are also very much influenced by our senses, which in turn affect our first impressions. What does your environment smell like? There are various incense mixtures that are said to be conducive to the mystical experience, such as frankincense and myrrh, as well as sensual oils that are known to have a calming effect. Some tarot readers actually perfume their decks. Many specialist vendors can provide "divination" incense and scented oils.[19] However, be aware that not all your clients will appreciate or can tolerate strong scents because of allergies or other health reasons. This is worth checking in advance.

If you know ahead of time the nature of the querent's question, you can use scents that correspond with it. For example, if the question is about love, rose petal incense would be recommended. If the question is about spiritual purpose and development, choose frankincense, which corresponds with spiritual elevation.

Ritual and Rites

There are many grounding rituals, protection rituals, and other preparatory rituals for magical work, if you consider tarot reading such a work. If not, there is little need for ritual unless you require some boundaries to be created with the other person. If you choose to use a ritual, it is up to you whether you want the client to witness it.

We use a simple invocation taken from the work of the Hermetic Order of the Golden Dawn:

I invoke thee, HRU, in the name of IAO, the great angel that is set over the operations of this secret wisdom, to lay your hands invisibly under these, my consecrated cards of art, that thereby we may obtain true knowledge of hidden things, to the glory of thy ineffable name.

We usually then "seal" the stacked deck by tracing with our finger a circle and a cross in the centre of it, representing the magical symbol of the rose and cross. We then tap it four times (for luck, perhaps, or perhaps to remind us that we are going to be reading in four different worlds) and present it to the client.

Sometimes we will say this invocation out loud; other times we will say it silently, which is okay so long as there is clear intention and a discernible change of state. We would like every reading to be considered a sacred moment, so we separate ourselves from mundane life with this invocation and small ritual.

Face-to-Face with the Client
The First Few Minutes

In the first few minutes of a reading, you are establishing the frame or context for what will take place in the reading session. This frame is an important point of the communication. As an example, if a reader said to you at the start of a reading, "There is nothing to be afraid of," that would probably make you wonder if there actually was something to fear! So we should come up with a good introduction to our reading, framed in a positive manner, stating how we will go about the reading itself and what the other person can expect.

It may be a little difficult to know what to say. One way to approach this is to ask previous clients these questions: "How would you describe your reading with me to a friend? What was it like for you? Did anything surprise you? Should I have done anything differently?" When you have a few answers, you can confidently build a statement to offer at the start of your reading, such as:

Many of those who have sought my readings have been surprised by how humorous it can be, even while discussing serious issues. I think that you will also enjoy my way of weaving stories into readings, particularly as I tend to describe cards in terms of modern films. I am hoping that, like most of my clients, you'll leave this reading not necessarily floating on a cloud, but certainly with a lot of new insight to help you move forward over the coming weeks.

You may be surprised by how your reading style appears to other people, which can be very different to the view from inside yourself. Get others to show you your own style, and then embrace it to present the cards' message clearly.

What to Do When You Flounder: The Four Levels Method

It happens to every reader some time—that panic-inducing moment when you don't have a clue what to say during a reading. Here we offer a simple technique for overcoming this situation.

Kabbalah, as mentioned earlier, is a system of Jewish mysticism, and its Tree of Life diagram is familiar to most esoteric students. In this system, when one studies a sacred text, there are four levels of interpretation. These levels of interpretation also apply very well to tarot:

1. Peshet: Simple
2. Remez: Symbolic
3. Drosh: Extended
4. Sod: Secret

The first level is the simple description of the text: its length, number of words, any key appearance of particular words, and so forth. In tarot, this is the simple and literal description of a card. Try it with this card, starting sentences with "I see…"

Notice that you automatically tend to "drift up" a level to the interpretative or symbolic level. You might say, "I see five men arguing," whereas what you actually see is only "five men holding sticks"—the "argument" is an interpretation of the literal images of the card.

So the next level is this symbolic one, where books of symbols can assist you, as well as any text written by the artist(s) and/or designer(s) of

5 of Wands
(The Universal Tarot)

the deck. At this level we say, "On this card are five staves, symbols of the will or values of a person."

The third level is "extended." In Kabbalah, we would look at other sacred texts, make comparisons, and put the studied text into a wider context. In tarot, we do this when we say such things as "So it is like a war…" or "This reminds me of the story of 'The Three Little Pigs.'" We're putting the card into a wider context, or translating it into a metaphor to make it more understandable. We also do it when we extend our interpretative level to the other person's life or our own, such as, "So in your life, this card represents those moments when you feel out of control or at a loss."

We reach the fourth or top level when we have those magical moments of connection or insight, intuition or conscious realisation, and there is a certain sense of "fit" in the reading. This is that "aha!" moment, when we suddenly understand the above card in the context of the spread: "So what is really happening is that your previous failures have led you to develop a bad habit, entirely self-destructive, where you never complete anything."

We have watched many hundreds of readers flounder at one time or another, and we know what happens: they almost always go *up* the levels of interpretation, usually straight to the symbolic. When they do so, often they fall back on clichés and sayings that don't really mean much, such as, "So here we can see that, like in 'The Three Little Pigs,' the wolf is not able to use his breath to blow the stone house down…" and so on. This does not help the other person.

The best way to deal with a moment of confusion is to go straight back *down* the levels to the absolute literal. Face the card and let it face you; reestablish your connection on the most basic level. Simply describe what you are seeing in the card. Keep describing, keep talking, and you will find that your intuition begins to flow again. At some point, you will naturally start to rise back up the levels, and there will have been no break in your reading. Also you will have remained true to the cards.

Here is an example with the above card in a "future" position in a spread:

So… er… I am seeing these five men. They are bearing their staves. One man is looking away whilst the others are looking in other directions. The sky is white. The man looking away is perhaps the leader—ah—so I figure that one particular experience or value in your future is being turned away because of the blankness of your memory, you have forgotten something that is most important to you …

And off you go again, back up the levels. So always remember: when stuck, face the card.

Before we leave this section, notice that the first letters of the Hebrew words for the levels spell out PRDS. Since Hebrew has no vowels, this may not be obvious at first as a word; however, it is the word "pardes," meaning "garden." We are more familiar with it when pronounced and spelt "paradise." So the Four Levels Method we showed you for tarot is actually the Kabbalah "Formula of Paradise" and is a way of opening the secrets of holy texts and reentering paradise. As our tarot is also, in a sense, a divine text, it is a key to that same garden.

The Final Few Minutes

When summing up your reading, we suggest that you allow five minutes for questions and discussion; however, do ensure that the five minutes is part of the measured time for the whole reading. Do not let the post-reading conversation drift into a long discussion where you have less control of the communication and may find yourself offering personal advice from your own viewpoint, whilst the other person is still in the "frame" of taking consultation.

You may also choose to ask clients to repeat back some of what they have gained from the reading, and check that they appear to understand what you have offered. Don't forget to ask how they found the overall experience so you can weave this into your opening statement, as we looked at earlier.

At the conclusion of the reading, offer your business details for further contact (including a business card, if you use one), ask if they would consider recommending you to others, and leave them with a small parting blessing statement, such as ours: "May a full deck of possibilities be yours."

Preparing for Questions
Outside of the Reading Itself

There are many questions you may be asked that are not part of the reading itself. Some will be questions about tarot, while others may be general questions about topics that people feel are associated with tarot. We have to prepare for these so we can face them with confidence. Here are some of the questions we are often asked at tarot conferences and workshops and by those coming to readings.

What Different Styles of Reading Are There?

This is an interesting question as it is rare to actually see other tarot readers reading in detail, or to have an explanation of their process. Marcus did this by having readings done for him over a period of two years in the late 1980s so he could experience multiple tarot readers and model their unconscious processes—a sort of mind-mapping of the reading process. Perhaps we could someday devise a questionnaire or list of observational points to slot readers neatly into a particular style.

There are no real, defined categories of reading styles, although there are plenty of reading methods—various spreads, the counting method, free-form reading, and so on. We offer here a *very* general typing of styles, to which you may wish to add your own:

- **Absolutely Predictive:** These are the readings that make statements such as "On Wednesday, a man named Ian and two friends will come calling for you with a legal offer."

- **Absolutely Empowering:** These are the readings wherein the reader shifts much or all engagement with the cards to the querent: "What do you see here in the Three of Wands?"
- **Absolutely Psychic:** Here the cards are used merely as a prop to psychic talent, so whilst the cards may be laid out, the reader might suddenly say, "I am getting the image of three men having an argument; it may be about you and something legal."
- **Absolutely Scientific:** Here the cards are read in a purely systematic style: "This card, the Three of Wands, corresponds with Binah in the world of Atziluth, so it means in this position that there will be a new formation of three things in a matter of values or law."

In our experience, we've found that most readers are not "absolutely" any one style, and overlap several if not all of the above categories. Some few readers also have their own unique style, such as Enrique Enriquez, whom we've dubbed "Absolutely Poetic."

There is perhaps also the style of "Absolutely Oracular," where the reader is totally inspired by the Divine. In the times of the ancient Greek oracles, this would be seen as a message directly from the gods and goddesses themselves, usually passed to the oracle through the god of divination, Apollo. Such messages are considerably more rare these days, although as discussed earlier, intuition may be seen as being divinely inspired.

What Should You Say if Someone Asks How Tarot Works, and Whether It Is Simply Random?

By the time you complete this book, you should have already prepared an "elevator pitch" (a stock answer) for the most frequent questions asked of tarot readers, such as this one (also see chapter 10). There is no one definitive answer; however, you can prepare your own personal reply along the lines of a metaphor. Marcus uses this:

Imagine that there is a pool of water into which every stone—every event, in time and space—is thrown. As the ripples of those stones interact, they create an almost infinite interference pattern. It is known from holography that if you flash-froze the water at any given moment, you could work out the location of all the stones from any segment of the ripples. Now imagine that the tarot reading is one of the stones, or an intersection of the ripples of every moment of your life and every possible moment of your life in the future. Because not only are all the stones dropped at once, every infinite combination of stones is also dropped in that moment—this is how the tarot works.

On the other hand, you can use a purely psychological model, such as, "The tarot works by providing images, in which our subconscious mind can perceive possibilities that may not have been apparent to our conscious mind."

How Does One Explain Psychic Perception or Intuition?

Again, you should have an elevator pitch prepared for this one, as you will be asked it often enough! We tend to think of intuition as "knowledge without knowing"—however, the topic has to be something about which do you have knowledge! For instance, a garage mechanic cannot intuit anything when faced with a complex cooking recipe, whereas a cook can intuit just the right thing to do to save a dish in danger, without knowing exactly why she has reached a particular decision. Similarly, a good tarot reader, with broad knowledge and experience, can intuit something in a reading without being able to tell how he has reached that conclusion.

Some people are naturally born with or develop (through strong early family experiences or traumatic events, for example) intuition about other people. When applied to tarot reading, this intuition can be a very powerful adjunct to their reading, so long as it is clear that the intuition has come from personal experience rather than anything in the cards. This, of course, is difficult if not impossible to separate, which is why the original question about intuition is difficult. You might want to do some brief research into what science says about psychic abilities and form your own conclusions.

———————

As you have seen in this chapter, there is no truly prescriptive way of reading tarot. We would be better served to find our own voice rather than trying to attain some perfect "one true way" of reading—one that simply does not exist. The cards have been around for many hundreds of years and their variations have hardly been touched; there are many secret combinations, chords, and rhymes to be sung from the deck and you are instrumental in sharing that song with others.

Five

Facing the Crowd: Reading for Parties and Groups

Over the last three decades, we have found that tarot is generally received openly and with enquiry by most people. We have not been subject to any negative press or public reaction, to our knowledge. This is partly because we always present tarot in an open and authentic spirit of interest, suitable for the audience. We never attempt to shock or mystify, to glamorise or apologise.

At one party, we did experience a totally unexpected reaction. Firstly, when someone asked about our profession and we started to explain a little bit about tarot, one person yelled out rudely, "Boring!" And so we decided to drop the subject. However, the partygoers, who were getting increasingly drunk, would not let it go. Later on that evening, two of them started smashing potato chips on the table and telling us, "Go on then, read them—read them!"

Whilst we declined to read the messy table, we made the point that we were tarot card readers and did not read chips—and neither did we read for chimps. As soon as it was practical and polite to do so, we left the party. We later learnt that this was a typical attack, not specifically on tarot but on anything that any so-called guest might have brought to the table that was not of interest to the hosts.

The moral of this story is that you cannot read for chimps, and neither should you automatically assume that it is tarot, or you personally, that is under attack.

In this chapter, we will look at ways of adding tarot into a party, gathering, or other social occasion; we will also share a number of fun and engaging games for use with other tarot enthusiasts. They will teach you about each other, and the tarot, at the same time as a lot of laughter goes on!

Incorporating tarot into a social scene can be a rewarding experience, although it can often be a fraught one if certain rules are not followed. We will start by laying out these rules of engagement, which as ever are based on our years of experience.

The Rules of Tarot Reading at Parties or for Groups

Never read for someone in front of other people, even if they have given permission

Whilst this may seem unnecessary, we ask that you trust us on this one: the cards can be very capricious, particularly when given an audience. Once Marcus was reading at a local fair when three young men and two young women came to his table. The youngest woman asked for a reading, and the others—to get their value—decided to listen in, with much joking and the permission of the woman getting the reading.

She asked the usual question, "What is going to happen with my relationship?" However, the object of her relationship was standing next to her. This should have raised an alarm; however, Marcus decided to press on with the reading. It had been a long day for no reward, so his mood was not the best—another warning sign.

As the reading progressed, it became apparent—and Marcus said so—that the relationship was very passionate, very physical, and very intense because of issues of control and dominance. This brought a great deal of blushing from the woman asking the question, and laughter from her friends. However, her partner was looking somewhat confused: this did not seem to be his experience of the relationship at all.

This was because—as Marcus again made clear from the cards—that the relationship being described by the cards was not with him: it was with someone else! At this point, in a scene that could have been a classic in any comedy film, everyone's eyes turned to one of the other young men in the group. It was immediately apparent that everyone other than the so-called partner (of course) had known for some time that the woman was carrying on another relationship with someone else in their group. Of course, this immediately led to a bit of a scuffle and they chased out into the field to continue their "discussion" of the reading.

This incident was more than enough to convince Marcus never again to read before a group. The point is: you do not know what the cards will say, and if it's something you cannot or should not say out loud, you will be placing yourself unnecessarily in a difficult situation.

Keeping the reading confidential—solely between the reader and querent, and the cards of course—also serves to preserve the mystery of tarot. This face to face engagement is always a unique and special moment and should not be subject to distractions. One solution might be to make a recording (given provisos of privacy and data protection) to play for others, should the querent wish to do so.

Always set a time limit for each reading

It is best that you set a time limit for each reading to ensure that you do not disrupt the party or gathering too much, should the gathering not be a stated "tarot party." (There is nothing worse than becoming a "tarot bore.") If tarot readings are a planned part of the event, setting a time limit for each reading also ensures that more partygoers are able to have one. Offering readings at a gathering only to disappoint several people who don't get the opportunity is perhaps worse than not doing the readings in the first place.

You should also ensure the time is limited so that you can deal with any unexpected emotional issues arising from a reading (such as crying, shock, surprise, or outright joyous laughter) on the part of the querent.

Arrange for and take payment in advance

This saves trouble and potential embarrassment later on and gets the matter out of way, allowing you to concentrate on reading the cards and the guests to enjoy the readings. You should also have presented your terms and conditions (see our website at www.tarotprofessionals.com for professional membership where we supply a template of terms and conditions, in addition to a code of professional conduct and standards).

Agree on attendance numbers in advance

In practice, the main thing to remember with parties is often they have been arranged by one person and not everyone has the same beliefs about tarot. You may find that the number of attendees wanting a reading varies as people make up their minds, even during the event itself. Ensure that you have received a fixed payment. You can also make a small presentation before commencing readings to put people's minds at rest and take general and common questions. This can be used to excite or calm the atmosphere in preparation for your style of reading.

Understand the environment

A hen-party is different than a stag-party. A private party in a mansion is different than a bar-gathering. You can often "case the joint" in advance and use the setting to your advantage. Also ensure that alcohol does not impair your enjoyment—whether drunk by others or yourself.

Methods and Activities
for Reading at Parties or for Groups

After introducing yourself as a tarot reader at parties or other social events, you will often be asked to perform a reading. If the conversation turns to previous bad readings or negative experiences that people have had with tarot, now is your chance to offer a positive engagement with the cards.

However, there may not be a place for a standard "across the table" reading, so we will discuss various methods of reading face to face, no matter what the circumstances. These have all been road-tested and tweaked over the years, so all you need is your deck to hand and a selection of methods from this toolkit.

The Oracular Sentence Method

This method is fun for lighthearted gatherings, New Year's Day celebrations, birthdays, and other occasions where passing yourself off as a living oracle can be done in a semi-humorous way. It can even be hammed up, if you are so inclined, for Samhain/Hallowe'en parties. However, do not be fooled: this method can provide powerful oracular advice for its recipients, who can be "warned" that they must approach the oracle with some trepidation.

Divide your deck in advance into three piles: majors, minors, and court cards. Place the piles face-down, from left to right, on your table. They will form the structure of an oracular sentence composed of a noun (a major arcana card), a verb (a minor arcana card) and an adjective (a court card). You may wish to practice this method and incorporate your own variations.

Invite participants to come to you to receive your oracular insight. Tell them that they will be receiving a memorable message from the cards themselves, although it might be cryptic. The important thing is that it is a message that the cards have for them personally at this time.

Ask the participant to shuffle each of the three decks, keeping them face-down.

Select the top card from the first pile, the majors. Turn it over and say in your most oracular voice the name of the card. If, for example, you turn over the Tower, simply say "the Tower." If you are moved in the moment to say something else, do so—however, for the method to work, it must be a noun (a name, an object, a thing). In this example, you might say "the change" or "the broken building." *Never deny an oracular moment; always say what feels true to you.*

Now select a card from the second pile, the minor cards. This card (verb) says what the previous card (noun) is doing. For instance, if we pulled the Three of Cups, you might say "dances." Add this verb to your noun and say it out loud, clearly and deliberately: "The Tower dances…" or "The change dances…"

Finally, select the top card from the third pile, the court cards, which gives you the adjective or descriptive word for how the action is being performed. If you drew the Queen of Cups, you might say "reflectively" or "dreamily."

You can now utter the full oracular sentence in your best soothsaying voice: "The change dances dreamily…" At this point, if you feel moved to do so, add any poetic or divinatory statement that comes to you, such as: "The change dances dreamily, and what falls shall come to the dance if you have patience."

The Tower, 3 of Cups, Queen of Cups (The Universal Tarot)

As an advanced version of this method, you can perform this reading by taking the top cards from each pile as already described, then adding "but…" and taking the bottom three cards as a prophetic warning.

One recent performance of this method at a gathering produced what turned out to be a very meaningful oracle, off-the-cuff, when the following cards were drawn for a participant:

The oracular sentence was given as: "The Sun dances playfully, but the Moon stabs deliberately…"

The participant heard this as "the son" rather than "the sun" and it immediately gave her a revelation with regard to a family situation that had been troubling her. The fact that "the moon" was doing the "stabbing" very "deliberately" confirmed something very powerfully for her.

It is surprising how we can create such oracular moments in the most unlikely circumstances.

Telling a Person's Story Method

When you don't have space to lay down your cards—for instance, if you are standing up talking to somebody—and still wish to give them a demonstration of a reading, you can use this method, which forms a narrative or story for the person. In effect, it is a light version of the Golden Dawn's "Opening of the Key" method, only a thousand times quicker. It builds on your earlier practice with storytelling (see chapter 2).

Top row: The Sun, 3 of Cups, and Page of Wands
Bottom row: The Moon, 10 of Swords, Queen of Wands (The Universal Tarot)

The advantage of this method is that you don't need to lay down your cards anywhere to perform it, thus can be done standing, like on a bus, on a train, or in a queue.

Ask the participant for his name (if you don't already know it), and then ask, "If your life were a book, what would the present chapter be called?" While this seems a fairly simple question, it is packed with deeper meaning and impact. The person may simply shrug and say "chapter 25" because he is aged twenty-five, or may give you a more revealing phrase such as "Falling Apart" or "A Time of Boredom." Already you have, very simply, given his unconscious an empowering suggestion: that his life can be seen as a story in a book, with its own narrative flow, plot, challenges, and layers of meaning. By using such a familiar metaphor, we can bring tarot into an immediate and relevant engagement with popular culture outside of its usual boundaries in the gypsy fortuneteller's booth.

Acknowledge his statement, and then say, "So if your life is now 'chapter 25,' who are you in the story?"

Shuffle the deck. Give it to the participant face-up. Now ask him to go through the deck, keeping it in order, to find the card that most feels like his image of himself in his life story. This may be any card—major, minor, or court. Whichever one he selects, this is his significator. This participation allows him to feel engaged in the reading.

Take back the deck and look at the two cards on either side of the significator. These two cards refer to the recent past of the participant that has led him to this present chapter. Briefly tell him what the cards say to you.

Then return the deck to the participant and ask him to shuffle it. You may say, "Let's see what's coming up in the next chapter..."

When he has shuffled, take the deck back, turn it face-up (if it isn't already), and quickly go through the cards until you locate the significator. Read the two cards above and below it as the "next event" in the person's life.

You can now steer this method in any direction to suit the time and circumstances. If the person wishes to ask a question about the "next chapter," allow him to do so whilst shuffling the deck; then chase the significator down and read the two cards on either side of it. If he wants to know about a specific aspect of his life—the following "chapters" or anything else—apply the same method.

Impromptu Card Method

Another useful one-card method for reading for the general public in a social setting is the "Impromptu" method. It works very well with sceptics and those casually interested.

Shuffle the deck and ask the person to select a card. Ask them to look at it.

Regardless of the amount of interest they show in the card, ask them, "Does that mean anything to you?" No matter what their response, unless it is a strong affirmative, ask them to return the card to the deck, saying, "No, that's not the card, then."

Repeat this as many times as necessary until they find a card that holds meaning to them. Then interpret that card for them, encouraging the to participate in the interpretation. If they continue to show a lack of engagement, simply conclude by saying, "The cards have no message for you at this time."

Activities for Tarot Enthusiasts

While the previous activities were directed toward a tarot card reader doing informal readings in a social setting, those that follow are more suitable for gatherings of tarot enthusiasts and students. Many of them are based on oracular games constructed by leading astrologer Lyn Birkbeck.[20]

The "What's Going to Happen?" Game

This game challenges you to read for other people in a group and not get too panicked about your ability to read the cards—it is good to play this game as both a beginner and an expert!

A timekeeper is required. Lay out the tables, ideally in two facing lines, to ensure you can move around.

Facing each other in pairs, you quickly choose who is going to be reader and who querent. The querent always asks the same question, "What's going to happen?"

Each reader takes three or four cards, as they wish, and reads them without positional meaning. The cards may suggest a time sequence, an overall meaning, or a simple sentence. Just make it up based on what you see.

The timekeeper allows just three minutes for the readings, then yells, "Change!" He or she can also use a klaxon, whistle, or bell.

Everyone on one side of the tables moves down one seat; those who have been readers switch to the role of querent, asking the same question and being read for in the same manner, for the same amount of time.

And verily is this like speed-divining. Have fun, make friends, don't get too invested in the reading, and you may find words as sweet as honey even as you exhaust yourself.

Resolve a Family Issue Activity

Pull the court cards out of the deck before starting and set the rest of the cards aside. Ask the group if anyone has a family issue or argument that they would like to have clarity on. Ask this querent to think of the issue while shuffling the cards, then instruct her to look at them and pick out one from each suit. Read the cards in the context of the family issue.

Alternately, you can ask the members of the group to anonymously write down a question on a slip of paper and drop all the slips into a bowl. Ask one of the members to draw a slip out of the bowl at random, and then draw cards for the answer or resolution.

Oracular Poetry Activity

This fun activity can be used as a tool for tarot exploration in person with a group of friends, or online with your tarot social network. You will need pen and paper and the twenty-two major arcana cards.

Separate the majors from your tarot deck and set the other cards aside. Shuffle the cards, then ask someone to begin by choosing a card. In our example, we will choose the High Priestess. Instruct that person to hold the High Priestess card, clear his mind of any thoughts except what he sees in it, and then introduce himself to the card, either out loud or silently. Next, tell him to ask for a sentence or phrase of wisdom. Allow a moment or two for him to meditate on the card and allow the muse to speak through him. Once the person feels he is done, have him write the sentence or phrase at the top of a piece of paper, and then fold it over to conceal the message.

The tarot card and folded paper is then passed to the next person, who follows the same procedure. Keep passing around the paper and card until everyone has had at least one turn at saying what they think the High Priestess card is seeing, speaking, and sharing with the group.

The following was revealed to a group of four after going around the circle twice:

- I am the High Priestess; I sit between two worlds. I watch and patiently wait for the time when I can reveal the secrets of what lies behind me and beyond me.
- She is mysterious and enigmatic and knows the secrets of the sea.
- Pomegranates and pillars, veils and vision.
- I see her stare at me silently.
- The secrets that I bear within weigh me down.
- The ocean is as deep as it is wide and vast.
- I ate the seeds of creation to transform the world above and below.
- She wants me to bear her mystery.

Use your intuition to make sense of the message. Alternately, you can have each person draw a fresh card for inspiration, rather than passing the same card around.

Name That Card Activity

This activity is meant to hone your observational skills, and is directed toward experienced tarot readers. It helps people become more familiar with the cards in a fun and informative way. We suggest starting with the Rider-Waite-Smith deck, which is well known to most readers. Once you get the hang of it, try it with other decks.

Blindfold one member of the group and place a tarot deck in her hands. Instruct her to shuffle the deck, take out a card, and hold it up to the group. The other members of the group take turns saying what they see on the card, while the blindfolded person must guess it based on the clues given.

Let's use the Knight of Pentacles as an example. Here are some typical responses:

- The card has a yellow background
- Rolling hills in the background
- Red glove
- Suit of armour
- Pentacles

To make a contest of it, have each blindfolded participant state, before starting, how many clues they will need in order to guess the card, kind of like the old "Name That Tune" game. See how many turns it takes for you to become better acquainted with your deck of choice.

Alphabet Tarot Activity

Take a card from the deck and hold it up to the group, for example, the Queen of Cups.

Choose a person to start with the first letter of the alphabet, A, and give a word beginning with A that describes the card. The next person will describe the card using a word beginning with B, and so on:

The Queen of Cups (The Universal Tarot)

    A: Amorous

    B: Bountiful

    C: Crestfallen

    D: Deliberation

    E: Elegant

    F: and so on…

Just a Minute Activity

Draw a card randomly. Each person has to talk for one minute about that card without using the same word twice, pausing, or getting off track about the theme of the card. You might want to define how long a pause is acceptable, such as more than five seconds. The first person in the group to catch the speaker repeating words, pausing longer than five seconds, or going off topic then takes over the subject. Alternately, each person can draw a new card when it's his turn to speak.

Five Things Activity

Each person is instructed to pick a theme or concept, and to choose five cards from his or her deck that correspond to these things. Don't choose randomly; look at the cards and choose based on their images, symbolism, or meaning. Give the others a spoken clue and show them the cards one by one. The object is to guess the theme or concept. The first person to guess correctly then takes his or her turn.

For example, let's use the concept "holidays" ("vacations" to you Americans). What ideas do you associate with a holiday or vacation? They might include taking a rest, getting away from the stresses of life, traveling to new places, spending special time with family and friends, enjoying good food and drink, and doing fun activities.

A spoken clue for this example might be, "Most people do this particular thing once a year."

Give this learning game a go, and you will be pleasantly surprised by how quickly your knowledge of the cards increases.

Liar's Tarot Activity

This game is for an intermediate group that knows a little about tarot. Draw a card and describe it for the rest of the group to guess—but feel free to sneak in a fib about its meaning. Say, for instance, that the card is the Page of Pentacles. You might say, "I am a page; I am young, enthusiastic, and proud of what I am. I am fast to invest. I have ambition and dreams of what lies beyond."

The group responds by calling out "truth" or "lie." Once somebody has spotted a lie, he or she takes over with a new card, and so on.

Tarot Truth or Dare

In a simple variant on the old game of "truth or dare," participants draw a card and someone else in the group gives them the choice of truth or dare. The truth or dare has to be relevant to the card chosen; so for example, a dare based on the Eight of Wands might be to send a prank text or e-mail to a close friend, or a suggestive one to a romantic interest, as suggested by the group!

Tarot Card Charades Activity

This is for experienced readers who will have to mime a reading using one to three cards, dependent on their skill level, within a three-minute period, until competing teams correctly guess the cards involved. You can simplify this game by using only majors, only minors, or only court cards, or even just the minor cards of one particular suit. There is only one rule: you cannot simply hold up the number of fingers for the number on the card and then mime a pentacle, cup, sword, or wand in the air!

———

We hope this chapter encourages you to find fast, fun, and friendly ways of introducing tarot into social events and gatherings. With a few common-sense rules and simple methods, you can easily share tarot with just about anyone, in all kinds of circumstances.

Six

Facing the Outside World: Tarot for Engaging Life

When we were preparing this book, Marcus went out for a walk with his wife to run through the "Tarot Walk" exercise you will find in this chapter. It had been several years since he had performed it, so he was keen to revisit it.

He chose the World card to explore, and started the walk from the local lakeside where a large carved hand, bowled to collect leaves and natural items, is placed. He looked around from that location for something "world-like" and saw light glinting on dew on a leaf across the path. This attracted his attention, so he moved closer.

He looked around again for something "world-related" and saw a tree that looked like it was very ancient. He walked to that tree and repeated the process until he found himself back on the path.

When he turned to look for the next feature, he saw something glinting at eye level in a tree nearby. He walked toward it and was astonished to see a silver pentagram, no bigger than a quarter dollar, hanging from the tree. It was an earring. Marcus assumed that it had fallen on the path, and someone had discovered it and hung it in the tree in case its owner came looking for it. However, finding this ancient symbol hanging on a tree in the middle of nowhere was a remarkable ending to his shamanic walk.

The moral of this story is that the magic of the cards is built into the world and its events.

While the majority of this book is about reading for other people, in this chapter we will consider our own relationship with the Universe, and how tarot can deepen that relationship. We will look at different methods of using tarot to broaden your horizons, to get you thinking outside of the box, and to look at the world in different ways.

These methods are derived from shamanism, as well as other sources, so you may have encountered them or studied them in other contexts. If this is the case, you may wish to explore these methods afresh so that tarot can throw new light on your previous experiences.

These approaches include examples of physical, elemental, animal, planetary, and zodiacal applications of tarot to daily life, and you are encouraged to discover your own applications based on those given here.

The Tarot Walk

In this first experience, you will be brought face to face with the hidden archetypal forces of the Universe through the twenty-two major arcana cards. Each time you practice it, you will be building up a set of living correspondences that will further your understanding of the deck, as well as your ability to offer guidance to others through your readings.

You can easily spend from an hour or two to half a day on this method, so allow plenty of time. You'll need a notepad and pen (or an iPad or similar device) and suitable clothing for the outdoor conditions, as you're about to go out and about. However, you can start this exercise from wherever you wish.

We'll start with the Magician card as our guide. Take it from your deck and look around your present location, be it indoors or out. Look for whatever feels or seems closest to the nature of the Magician. This can be obvious or subtle; for example, you might see a t-shirt with "Magic" written on it, or a pen, which is appropriate for the Magician as a scribe or communicator.

The Magician
(The Universal Tarot)

Walk to the location of the object, make a note of it, and then have a look around from this new location (even if it's only a few steps away). Again, look for something that reminds you of the Magician. This might be, for instance, a stick shaped like a wand that you can now see out your window. Make your way to that object, make a note of it, and then do the same thing again.

You can perform the walk for a set amount of time, or until you come across an object that you feel truly represents the nature of the card. You can keep going until you find a natural object you can take from its location easily, or you can discover and purchase a stone, a book, or an item of clothing in a shop. If you like, you can add the items from your tarot walks to your altar. If you are artistic, you can create a new version of the card from the components of your journey.

Each time you return to the Tarot Walk exercise, choose a different major arcana card to explore. Eventually, you will create your own table of correspondences for each of them. Furthermore, when you next perform a reading and a major arcana card shows up, you will have a more intimate relationship with the energy of the card and a more personal experience of the manner in which these twenty-two archetypal energies appear in our daily life.

Here are some of the qualities and objects or locations you might associate with each card.

Card	Qualities of the Card	Associated Objects and Locations
0: The Fool	Comedy, freedom, weirdness, the unusual	A toy clown, a strange piece of music, a key, a small dog
1: The Magician	Magic, invention, trickery, communication	A wand, a pen, a satellite dish, a communications cable
2: The High Priestess	Mystery, revelation, secrets, the veil between worlds	A curtain, a border crossing, objects associated with the occult, a book, tall pillars
3: The Empress	Growth, cultivation, nature, motherhood, harvest	A pregnant woman, a nest, a garden
4: The Emperor	Fatherhood, rulership, law, control	A policeman, a crown, a sign saying "do not ..."
5: The Hierophant	Religion, values, tradition, teaching	A library, a Bible, a church, a school, a cross
6: The Lovers	Choices, love, inspiration	A pair of lovers or birds, a Rose Key, a T-shaped junction in the road, two paths splitting in a wood, a romantic card
7: The Chariot	Balanced movement and stillness, being in the flow	A toy car, a vehicle or cart, a spinning top or gyroscope, a sphinx
8: Strength	Right relationship, harmony, balance, perfected control	A lion, a pulley held in balance, a strong person, somebody standing up for themselves
9: The Hermit	Guidance, illumination, teaching by example	A lamp, a staff, a high path, a sign, a lighthouse

10: The Wheel of Fortune	Cause/effect, cycles, chance, changes in rotation	A wheel, a bicycle, an elevator, games of chance
11: Justice	Balance, law, rightness	Scales, a sword, a blindfold, a courthouse, an attorney
12: The Hanged Man	Suspension, higher values, sacrifice	A gent's tie, a spider in a web, dew hanging on a tree
13: Death	Transformation, change, elimination	A coal in a fire, a dead insect, a fossil, something broken made into something new
14: Temperance	Tempering, patience, combination	A cake, a recipe, a cocktail
15: The Devil	Attachment, ignorance, reversed or blinded perception	A bicycle lock and chain, a padlock, a trailer hitched to a vehicle, a goat or other animal with horns
16: The Tower	Sudden change, acceleration	Lightning, a bright flash or sudden shock, a practical joke, a ruined building
17: The Star	Vision, hope, a guide	A star in any form, a twinkle of light in a mirror
18: The Moon	Fear, illusion, dreams, the unconscious	An incense-filled room, a piece of silver, a sign saying "dream"
19: The Sun	Expansion, light, success	The sun, a piece of gold, a smiling face
20: Judgement	Decision, calling, resurrection	An unexpected call or visit, a party invitation
21: The World	Synthesis, wholeness, completion	Nature, all four elements, the last piece of a jigsaw puzzle

The Tarot by Wind and Water

When reading for yourself, it can be difficult to know whether you are over-interpreting a card or a spread to suit your own preconceptions. In this method, we allow the world of the elements to assist us.

The Tarot by Wind

You will require ten helium balloons, easily available from most party supply shops, ten stamped postcards, and a "throwaway" tarot deck (perhaps a mini-deck), since you may never get all the cards back. You may also use photocopies of the tarot cards rather than the actual cards.

Take the deck you'll be using and shuffle whilst asking your question. Lay out ten cards in the Celtic Cross pattern.

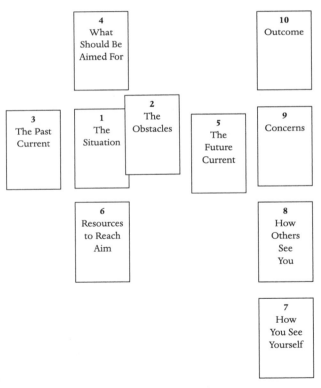

The Celtic Cross Spread

Number the cards in permanent marker on their backs, and then fasten one to each of the ten balloons. Write on all ten postcards your name and address, and a request to return the postcard (not the tarot card) with WHERE the balloon was found, and any message from the finder with regard to the tarot card. Fasten the postcards to the balloons. Await a good breeze and then release the balloons to the sky and to the wind.

The returned cards can be read in the sequence they are returned, or by their original positions on the Celtic Cross, and with additional interpretations based on their found locations or written response from the finder.

If you are wary of sending out tarot cards, you can also perform this method by choosing ten postcard images that are close to the ten tarot cards you have picked, fastening them to the balloons, and asking what the image means to the finder.[21]

The Tarot by Water

You can use the element of water in a similar way by placing the cards in bottles and casting them into the sea or a swiftly flowing river or stream.

The Tarot Shaman's Path

Whilst there is no specific connection between shamanism and tarot, many of the methods and approaches found in shamanistic practice can be applied to deepen our experience of the cards in a profound and practical way.

This method uses the concept of gated spreads, introduced in *Tarosophy*. These are spreads done over a period of days, where each spread is reliant not only upon the previous spread, but also on actions carried out in real life (and arising results), which feed into the next spread. Thus a series of "gates" is created, through which the activity of life is channelled. As the cards represent fundamental patterns in life, this channelling can produce profound, life-changing effects. It is a way of experiencing firsthand that the world is indeed bound by invisible knots.

In this activity, we are going to follow the path of the tarot shaman into the animal symbolism of tarot and engage with the life force surrounding us. This may be a powerful week for you; whilst writing this, Marcus looked out the library window and saw a deer staring back at him. You may also like to record your dreams during this time, since they may become more vivid.

In *The Teachings of Don Juan*, Carlos Castaneda gives an account of the requirements of the shaman, the Person of Knowledge. The shaman must:

1. Be learned
2. Be of unbending intent
3. Be clear of mind
4. Be laborious
5. Be a warrior
6. Be unceasing
7. Possess an ally

The Tarot cards of the Magician, the Chariot, the Hermit, Strength, the Emperor, and the Wheel of Fortune symbolise the archetypal qualities of the first six requirements, but we also need to locate our ally. To do so, we must encounter the Dweller on the Threshold—the Guardian of the Gate.

You may note in your journal which cards you personally see associated with the first six qualities.

Gate 1: The Guardian of the Gate Spread

Our first gated spread tells us what we must overcome to go on to the next gate; it is a warrior's challenge. We cannot even begin to approach the mysteries unless we prove ourselves worthy.

Take a deck and shuffle, considering everything that frightens you, then lay out three cards in a line (vertical or horizontal) as follows:

1. What is the Guardian?

2. How must I fight?

3. What is the reward?

Consider how these cards might relate to your life over the next day. What is the nature of your fear that has been divined by the first card? What is the manner in which you must overcome this fear, as indicated by the second card? And what does the third card suggest you will gain as a reward?

- Guardian: The Tower
- Fight: Ace of Swords
- Reward: The Empress

In this example, the Guardian card could be read as a fear of disruption and sudden failure. The Fight card could be read as the need to hold fast to one's ideas, while the Reward card could be read as an increase in personal growth (or creativity) if this challenge is met. Some area of your life will clearly relate to the message of these three cards.

Next, and most importantly, decide on a definite action you will take in the next twenty-four hours that will satisfy the requirements of this gate. Don't feel you need to do something dramatic—unless, of course, you feel called to do so.

So to continue with our example, tomorrow we will try to do something that relates to the world of ideas. We'll overturn an expectation and overcome a barrier by starting to write an essay we have been prevaricating over. It's not much of a challenge in terms of being a warrior, but it must be done. The Ace of Swords cuts through our procrastination, and our reward will surely be an exceptionally creative piece of writing!

You are encouraged to share your decisions, actions, and experiences on our tarot forum. We have found that sharing often reveals profound similarities and interesting differences in the lives of those participating.

Gate 2: The Journey

Having overcome the Guardian, next we'll go on a journey to prepare ourselves to meet our animal guide. Of course, we must travel, but we must also do so with a relaxed attitude—the world is closer to us than we imagine. There is a great scene in a book based on a reimagining of Anglo-Saxon shamanism, *The Way of Wyrd* by Brian Bates, where the shaman is taking a student through an exercise. He says, "Relax! You are tying yourself in knots with tension. Relax and your Guardian Spirit will cut through the fog of your life like a sunbeam." He then jokes that the student must have been chosen by an owl guardian, since he is looking so wide-eyed and intent! Humour is an important part of shamanistic training, as is trickery. So on our second day on the path of the tarot shaman, our shaman will take us on a dance…

Yesterday our first gated spread told us what we must overcome to make progress, and we acted upon this divination today. By now you will have received the reward indicated by the spread, or at least deepened your appreciation of what holds you back from progress.

For the second gated spread, you will need your deck and a small notebook and pen or pencil, plus suitable clothing for the weather conditions and environment in which you are situated, because you may be going outside.

Shuffle your deck considering all the journeys you have been upon—literal or metaphorical. Consider what you learnt, who you saw, what you recall. When you are ready, stop shuffling and take the top card from your deck. We do not use reversals (upside-down cards) in this particular spread.[22]

Make a note of the card in your notepad, and perhaps a brief note (to be expanded later) as to what it tells you about journeys. For example, we pulled the Knight of Cups from Roxi Sim's Pearls of Wisdom deck. The Knight tells us that the journey should always be full of delight, and not to miss the opportunity to go on detours to interesting places along the way!

Now, make a journey—even if it is only into another room in the house, or outside, based on the card you drew. For instance, we chose to go into the kitchen, because of its association with the suit of cups. When you are in that new location, choose the next card, and do the same as before. We got the Knight of Swords, which says we must be prepared for a journey and prepared to cut through things quickly. So we simply walked across to the drawers and picked out a small, blunt knife.

Continue to work through the cards, taking either small steps around your house and yard, or actually walking or driving to farther destinations, and picking up items along the way.

Stop when you reach a place or lesson from the cards that just feels right. (If you are in any doubt, it is not the place.) Make a note of the final card you received that brought you to this place or taught you this particular lesson about journeying. You may have pulled three cards and not left your house, or you may have pulled thirty cards and travelled a hundred miles in the day. It is your journey, and you will know what's right for you. You can read the accumulated cards as a spread, if you wish, or simply treat them as signposts on your journey.

Once you are at this end place or point, consider how far you have come since you started the journey. Consider what you learnt yesterday about your fears and what needed to be overcome. Now find your strength renewed in this place, which is a "power spot" as it is called in the works of Carlos Castaneda, who wrote about the Yaqui shaman Don Juan. Once you have completed this journey, you may return to this spot again, or it may just be a one-off visit. You can even make a map of the cards and the locations through which you have journeyed. We call this a geographical spread.

The symbolism of tarot is populated with animals—birds, reptiles, fish, and mammals, real and imaginary. A wonderful example of how these are used as complex symbols is the exquisitely named article, "The Aviary at the Gates of Heaven," which discusses the birds used on the Empress card in the Thoth Tarot. In the shamanic traditions, animals are seen as messengers and guides—spirits in their own right. Whilst we will examine this symbolism more tomorrow, today we are going to do a very simple exercise to summon our animal guide.

In this next gate, having proven ourselves and embarked on a journey, we will take our sacred place and summon a spirit of an animal from our tarot deck. First, we must have the animal choose us by consulting with what the Sufis call the Counsel.

Gate 3: The Summoning

Go through your deck and select out all the cards that have an animal on them. If you are using a pagan deck or animal oracle deck, this may be all of the cards! On the other hand, if your deck has no animals at all, please select an alternative deck.

Shuffle, and place these cards face-down about you, on the floor, in any pattern—perhaps a circle. Take any natural object, such as a crystal, stick, or stone, and place it at the centre of the spread.

Begin to move the object around, feeling it respond to the cards. When your sensation of calling or pulling or knowing is strongest, place the object upon that card. Leave it there. *Do not look at the card.* Put the other cards away.

Now spend the day wondering what the spirit of the card is. Try to perceive its calling or summoning in the activities of the day. For example, are you noticing squirrels everywhere you go? Or did a certain type of bird land on your windowsill? Encounters like these may be clues.

At the end of the day, you can write down your experiences and look at the card, comparing your impressions with the animal you see on the card.

Now we approach the last stages of our first experience of tarot shamanism. Today we are going to create a special *sigil*—magical symbol—to focus the energy of our animal. A spirit catcher is in some ways similar to a *veve* in Voodoo traditions or a talisman in the Western esoteric traditions. In a sense it is also a mandala. It is a physical representation that acts as a focus for the energies of the spirit. It can be used by placing it on one's personal altar, hiding it somewhere of import, or carrying it about on one's person. You may even wish to take this magical diagram to the place of power you discovered in the Journey gate and ritually burn it or bury it.

Gate 4: Creating a Spirit Catcher

Take your deck and shuffle it whilst considering the guardian you have overcome, the journey you took, and the animal that was revealed at the last gate. Concentrate on that animal and ask, "How may I honour your spirit?" Take out one card. Lay the card face-up and make a note of the key symbols, items, objects, and colours in each of the following areas of the card:

The Shaman Matrix

Suppose that the upper-left section of the card contains just sky. You could write in that section of the box, "blue" or "sky." Select the most prominent symbol in that area of the card *for you*, whilst also thinking of the animal.

Then imagine that this box represents a new spread. The top two sections are "How you honour me in your spiritual life," the middle two sections are "How you honour me in your thoughts and feelings," and the bottom two sections are "How you honour me in your daily activities." These are the three levels of the world.

Take each of the three symbols and read them as if they were very simple tarot cards. What comes to mind? Write down your feelings and impressions.

In this manner of reading, each individual card becomes a mandala. It is also a spirit catcher, in that for the next twenty-four hours you must live according to these divinations before completing the last gate. These activities honour your animal spirit in all levels of your life. You should also record any dreams or events of note during this time.

We come now to the final gate of this gated spreads experience. Here we pull together our experience by invoking, embodying, and being empowered by the animal spirit we have been called by, and which we have caught by honouring it.

Gate 5: Invocation of the Animal Spirit

This activity uses a variation of a magical practice taught by urban shaman and modern chaos magician Jan Fries, whose books I recommend, particularly *Visual Magick*.

On a largish sheet of paper, draw a rough sketch of your animal spirit. This can be stylistic, symbolic, or realistic. Draw a cross on five places on the sketch. These could be key features such as the eye, wing, tail, heart, and so on. Write in each position a phrase that is appropriate to that part of the animal: "This is the vision of my spirit," "This is the spiritual power of my spirit," "This is the heart of my spirit." Now take your deck and shuffle whilst contemplating the journey that has brought you to this place, the fear you had to overcome, the journey, the calling and the catching, and the honouring of your animal spirit. All the gates have led to this divine moment.

When you are ready, draw a card for each position on the animal. These cards represent the animal's response to you. They show how you can invoke the powers and qualities of your animal spirit. They tell you how to live the animal.

For example, if we had a bat as our animal, and we had placed a cross on its ear(s), we could write, "This is the secret sense of the bat, my spirit." Then we pulled the Seven of Disks (Thoth Tarot) in that position, which we would read as follows: "Failure and sloth—the secret sense of my animal spirit is present and invoked whenever I give up trying and relax, surrender."

You now have five points of invocation of your animal spirit. As a tarot shaman, you can use these cards to draw upon the power of your animal guide, perhaps leaving them visible by your bed before sleep and communing with your animal in dreams. You may also create a montage of the cards to represent your animal, or use them in some other way to remind you of all that you have learnt during this week.

The Tarot Week

When working with tarot to engage life, one method is to live a Tarot Week. We do this by using the magical correspondences of the major arcana, which are appropriate to the planets of the week. This series of cards takes us from the Sun lighting our way at the beginning, to the World where we come to rest. You should, of course, begin on a Sunday.

Day	Planet	Tarot Card
Sunday	Sun	The Sun
Monday	Moon	The High Priestess
Tuesday	Mars	The Tower
Wednesday	Mercury	The Magician
Thursday	Jupiter	The Wheel of Fortune
Friday	Venus	The Empress
Saturday	Saturn	The World

Let's take a look at how we can incorporate the cards' energy into each day of our Tarot Week, using a journal to connect the days together.

Sunday: The Sun—Day of Expression

The Sun is all about light. The god Apollo was not just a god of the sun, but of light generally. Our mystical path is full of allusions to and experiences of light; light is often seen as the divine, the spirit, and the creative force. In psychological terms, the Sun is the centre of the self, as it is of the astronomical solar system. It also relates to self-expression.

We will start the week by creating a "Freedom List" in our journal. This list is based on Aleister Crowley's *Liber Oz*, a statement of the rights of all persons. He stated that all people have the right to work, play, and rest as they will; to eat, drink, dwell, and travel as they will; to think, speak, write, draw, and create as they will. He also outlined a few more rights, some controversial; "to dress as you will" is one of the safe ones!

In your journal, write down what you feel free to do—where there are no constraints in your life. Consider the expansive sun, your solar self, and identify where you can shine. Write down only what accords with the sun—those freedoms—rather than your constraints, limitations, and blocks.

In itself, this can be an enlightening and even liberating experience. However, when used as the first step of a Tarot Week exercise, it can prove life-changing. In the example below, we show a few lines that should not be included in the journal as they are stated in the negative.

I am free to speak my own mind, and free to choose what to eat ~~other than too much sugar~~. I am free to read anything. I am free to choose what I do today ~~however I have to go to work tomorrow~~. I am free to wear what I wish, and free to cook anything I choose. I am able to walk wherever I want…

Continue on as much as you can to really capture the areas of life where you have the possibility of expansion. Focus entirely on the sun, the light, and the freedom of your life. At this stage we are not concerned about self-judgment, constraints, or other limitations that the exercise may highlight.

Next, carry out at least one activity today that you listed, in honour of the Sun tarot card. It can be as simple or extravagant as you wish; it just has to be carried out in the spirit of freedom and expansiveness. Even a person in prison can choose which of four walls he wishes to touch.

Monday: The High Priestess—Day of Mystery

On Sunday, we looked at our areas of freedom. These are navigated by our conscious will—our decisions to do one thing or another, within the illuminated chart of our freedom. Today we dive into deeper waters by performing a divination by tarot, honouring the High Priestess, to whom the moon is attributed in astrology, and whose day is Monday. The High Priestess is all about our intuition, the deeper currents that run through our life.

Perform a simple five-card tarot reading, drawing one card for today, Tuesday, Wednesday, Thursday, and Friday. Write down what immediately comes to mind for each card and how you would interpret that card as "telling a fortune" for each of these days. In other words, what do you think each day will be like, based on its card?

At the end of today and each following day, review the card and your experiences, and contemplate any connections between your divination and the day itself. As the days progress and your other Tarot Week work kicks in, the way you read each card may change from your original interpretation today, which you can note in your journal.

Here's an example of the card we pulled for Wednesday and our immediate interpretation:

Queen of Cups: On Wednesday, a gift of oracular nature will be delivered. It may be that a long-awaited dream will happen—which is possible, as this is the scheduled delivery date of a tarot book. We will also pay special attention to any message delivered to us by a woman with a kind and emotional nature.

Tuesday: The Tower—Day of Change

The Tower is one of the significant "change" cards in the deck. Whilst many of the cards deal with change in some way (and education, another common theme of the major arcana), this is one of the most immediate. It tells us that there is sudden change coming from outside of ourselves, and there is little we can do other than create new horizons out of the change.

For our Tarot Week activity for today, make a list of things you can change; in effect, this builds on our Sunday exercise. Here we see how we are free or constrained to affect our own life. The Sun shines, and the Tower strikes!

Next, do something to honour the Tower card and its planetary correspondence in our life by changing something today—deliberately and in full awareness. Again, it matters little whether it is a minor or major act, since sometimes even the smallest action can cause significant change.

For instance, we might write, "I can change my shoes, my hair, my desktop. I can change from drinking tea to drinking coffee. I can change someone's state by telling them a joke and making them laugh…"

We quite like that latter action, so it is the one we choose to do today. Also, don't forget to revisit Monday's prediction for today. Was it accurate? Write about it in your journal.

Wednesday: The Magician—Day of Magic

Wednesday corresponds to the Magician. As he can be a tricky character, we are going to honour him by performing a magical trick ourselves, using our tarot deck. There are many ways of going about this, so we have chosen a powerful yet simple ritual to engage everything we will do this week to effect elegant change.

Take the seven planetary Tarot cards (the Sun, the High Priestess, the Tower, the Magician, the Wheel of Fortune, the Empress, and the World) and lay them out, face-up, in this order. Now shuffle them and lay them out, face-down, in a line.

We'll now play a "Truth or Dare" game mixed with a "Find the Lady" game to engage our will and focus, the key components of the Magician card.

Move your hand across the seven face-down cards and say, "If I do not discover the Magician, I will…" and then state some "forfeit" or penalty activity you can carry out today; for example, you might choose "clear out the cellar." Lay your hand on a chosen card, turn it over, and see if you have discovered the Magician. If he shows up on your first pick, the Magician has blessed you to have a totally free day. Do what thou wilt!

If, however, you do not discover the Magician, leave the card chosen face-up and repeat the process, with another forfeit to be added to the first if you do not discover the Magician this time. Keep repeating the task until you have discovered the Magician, and then ensure you do the tasks, which are now magical acts of will. If you find your Wednesday focused on six magical tasks because the Magician hid from you for all your choices, then you have our sympathy—however, you will have truly experienced the correspondence of the card to the trickster Mercury.

We'll also return to our oracular prediction from Monday, in which we drew the Queen of Cups for today. As we reviewed today's events, we remembered that there was a nice lady in the bank who said to us, "It will stop raining by tomorrow." At the time, we didn't think much of this; however, in review we realise that she was the Queen of Cups—the mention of rain corresponding to the water of the suit of cups. Her message that it will stop raining soon, spoken as it was in a bank, could perhaps be interpreted as meaning that our finances will improve tomorrow. We will be able to check that.

Thursday: The Wheel of Fortune—Day of Flow

Whilst yesterday was about will and focus, with the Wheel of Fortune we take the more circular and interconnected concept of karma—cause and effect—by the scruff of its neck, so to speak, by engaging with risk and chance. We have used our week so far to explore issues of freedom and choice, along with mystery and magic. Today we throw caution to the wind and see what happens when we let ourselves go with the flow.

The task for today—and it may prove very restful, or otherwise—is to simply go along with whatever unfolds. Attempt to live in the moment, make no plans, hold no regrets. Be present as much as possible, and experience the day fully.

The Wheel of Fortune holds all possibilities, so you can decide at the start of today to simply accept everything that happens and take every opportunity that presents itself without consideration. Whilst this may be a risk (and it is entirely up to you to decide what risks to take in your life), if you approach it without preconceptions, it may prove very liberating.

A film like *Yes Man* (2008) shows one way of opening oneself to this concept, while *Groundhog Day* (1993) does so in a totally different manner.

Make a note in your journal how this Jovian Wheel day differs from the previous Mercurial Magician day, and begin to observe how all days vibrate between these two extremes, the "1" of the Magician and the "10" of the Wheel. There is a deeper Kabbalistic consideration in this relationship, which you have now experienced in your Tarot Week—how the 1 and the 10, the magical source and the wheel of manifestation—are connected.

Don't forget to revisit Monday's prediction for today and write about it in your journal.

Friday: The Empress—Day of Growth

The Empress is literally pregnant with potential, and symbolises natural growth, cultivation, care, motherhood, and the divine feminine. She is the womb and the matrix—the matter—of creation. So our Friday should be a day on which we celebrate our ability to nurture all that grows toward the light of the sun.

Today, take into consideration all that you are free to do, all that you have divined, all that you have changed. Consider also all that you willed, all that you accepted. Now, in the light of all that you have observed during your Tarot Week, choose one thing to grow and nurture. Perhaps you choose a relationship or a project at work; perhaps you choose to teach someone or to give a gift that furthers the personal growth of another person. It is up to you.

Make a note in your journal how this offering, this nurturing, enriches your life and how it connects to all that has preceded it in the week. You may see that the Empress unifies all the other cards, since she corresponds to Venus, the only one of the planetary symbols to fully embrace the whole of the Tree of Life.

Also, remember to revisit Monday's prediction for today and write about it in your journal.

Saturday: The World—Day of Engagement

On Saturn's day, before we return again to the light of pure awareness and freedom on Sunday, we consolidate and manifest our work. Saturn is seen as a planet of structure, tradition, and constraint. It can hold us back and challenge us, yet at the same time it rewards us by giving us things of the world—and it is the World card to which we come today. As it is a Saturday, it is quite appropriate that today is a very material day.

Today, enjoy the material world in some manner. Whether you go for a walk in the park or go shopping, get out and touch, smell, feel, and sense the world. Watch a movie, go out for a meal or cook one. Indulge yourself in our shared physical reality. This is the surface of the light that you experienced in the freedom exercise—and whilst it is engaging, it is also constraining; there are only so many things you can do. So enjoy what you can today, and make notes in your journal of your experience of the World.

How does it feel when you consider all that you are free to do, all that you have divined, all that you have changed, all that you willed, all that you have accepted, and all that you have nurtured? How have the experiences of your Tarot Week informed and shaped your relationship to the world?

With this summation, you have come to the end of the exercise. You can also continue it for one or more extra weeks, each time spiralling to new insights and conclusions, or revisit it every so often, perhaps once a year or once a season.

Optional Extras to your Tarot Week[23]

You can burn a candle at the start and end of each day, in a colour appropriate to the planet and/or tarot card of the day. This will help you focus and remain aware of the nature of the day's energy.

Sunday:	Orange or gold
Monday:	White or blue
Tuesday:	Red
Wednesday:	Yellow or orange
Thursday:	Blue or violet
Friday:	Green
Saturday:	Black or purple

You can also burn incense as appropriate to the planet and card:

Sunday:	Frankincense
Monday:	Myrrh, myrtle
Tuesday:	Lignum aloes
Wednesday:	Cinnamon
Thursday:	Nutmeg, saffron
Friday:	Rose
Saturday:	Storax

Tarot Currents

In this method of engaging life, we utilise the correspondences of the major arcana cards to the zodiac to align our own life with the tides of the sun and moon, thereby surfing their waves rather than having them crash over us.

You will need access to an almanac or a solar/lunar calendar, which are readily available on a number of astrology websites.[24] As the sun moves through one sign of the zodiac approximately every month (twelve signs for twelve months of the year) and the moon moves through a sign every two or three days (twelve signs each month), there are 12 x 12 = 144 combinations of this joint current. It is like a braid twisted from two fibres, which changes its quality every two or three twists.

So we can have the sun in Cancer on a date in July, with the moon in Scorpio for two days over that same date. After those two days, with the sun remaining in Cancer, the moon moves into Sagittarius. Later in the month, the sun shifts its position into Leo, whilst the moon continues changing sign every two or three days. There are some points in the yearly cycle when both the sun and the moon are in the same sign at the same time. This happens each month at the new moon, and can be seen in the almanac or calendar. (Each month at the full moon, the sun and moon are in opposite signs.)

So in this activity, we'll take the tarot cards corresponding to the signs in which the sun and moon are placed for any given day, and read them as a two-card combination that illustrates the underlying nature of that day. We can then align our activities to the prevailing energy, to best take advantage of these deeper currents.

As a simple rule, the card corresponding to the sign in which the sun is placed shows you what to be most aware of. The card corresponding to the sign in which the moon is placed shows you a personal reflection to consider.

Here are the astrological correspondences:

Zodiacal Sign	Card	Zodiacal Sign	Card
Aries	The Emperor	Libra	Justice
Taurus	The Hierophant	Scorpio	Death
Gemini	The Lovers	Sagittarius	Temperance
Cancer	The Chariot	Capricorn	The Devil
Leo	Strength	Aquarius	The Star
Virgo	The Hermit	Pisces	The Moon

We give below some examples that come from 2010.

• 23–24 July: Sun in Leo: Strength; Moon in Capricorn: The Devil.
  A tough time revealing what you cannot let go of—yet. A clue to a better relationship.

- 25–27 July: Sun in Leo: Strength; Moon in Aquarius: The Star. During the full moon on the 25th, be brave and listen to dreams. They are *yours*—align to them!
- 28–29 July: Sun in Leo: Strength; Moon in Pisces: The Moon. Reflecting on the strength of fear, you find the fear strengthens your resolve to fight.

––––––––––

In this chapter, we have covered many ways of engaging and enhancing daily life with the tarot. In this way we look to deepen our comprehension of our experiences on earth and connect to the magic and mystery of the invisible knots that bind the world and its people together.

§even

Facing Each Other: Tarot and Relationships

In the tarot are many cards dealing with relationship. In fact, all of them could be said to represent different faces of our relationship with the world. As such, they should encourage us to engage with the world rather than being used as an idle escape from it.

A few years ago, a client told Marcus that she wanted a male friend of hers to visit him for a reading. This went on for some months, with various cancelled appointments, and it seemed apparent the young man was in no mind to have a tarot reading done for him. Then, finally, Marcus received a phone call from the man, asking to have the reading the following day.

When he arrived, he was extremely nervous and looked exhausted. He sat down and, after Marcus introduced himself and his approach to tarot, motioned for the reading to carry on without him saying anything further. At this point, Marcus got a strong feeling that he should pass the entire deck to the man and not only have him shuffle it, but lay out the spread also. In his head was something about "give him the power."

The man shuffled the deck and, before laying out the cards for a spread, Marcus asked him to turn over the deck and look at the base card, which was "what is really going on for you." The man did this and looked astonished at the card he was seeing, then promptly burst into tears.

The card was the Three of Swords, the card of heartbreak, showing a heart pierced by three swords. As Marcus soon learned, not only was the man an absolute disbeliever about tarot, he had been going through an intense depression following a relationship breakup and had only finally come for the reading to stop his friend from harassing him.

The moral of this story is the cards don't know that you don't believe in them.

In this chapter, we focus on spreads and activities that relate specifically to our relationships.

The Marriage Cards Spread

We can use astrology to add another layer of meaning to our readings. Whilst this can be explored through other books, such as *Tarot and Astrology* by Corrine Kenner, here we give a method that "marries" your cards with those of another person. You can use it to check your compatibility or, for existing relationships, see how you can best fit your styles together. For this method, you will need to know your sun and moon signs[25] or your birth details so you can look up these important positions.

From your deck, take out as your significators the two cards that correspond to these two signs. If your sun and moon are both in the same sign, simply select the one card that corresponds to that sign for your significator. Here, again, are the astrological correspondences:

Zodiacal Sign	Card	Zodiacal Sign	Card
Aries	The Emperor	Libra	Justice
Taurus	The Hierophant	Scorpio	Death
Gemini	The Lovers	Sagittarius	Temperance
Cancer	The Chariot	Capricorn	The Devil
Leo	Strength	Aquarius	The Star
Virgo	The Hermit	Pisces	The Moon

Let's do an example. Brad Pitt has moon in Capricorn and sun in Sagittarius, so his two cards are the Devil and Temperance—an interesting combination, with the excesses of a devil-may-care attitude combined with the wonderful balancing of Temperance. We choose the moon sign first in this method because it has to do with the inner, emotional part of ourselves, which is then expressed in the outer world through our sun sign.

Now we can assign a "relating" phrase to marry these cards together, based on the keywords below. These were chosen for us by leading author and astrologer Lyn Birkbeck. Look at your moon sign and sun sign, and select the two keywords to which they correspond. This will result in a two-word phrase for your solar/lunar significators. You can practice with well-known celebrities or historical figures, where we have their birth details, such as William Shakespeare (Libra moon, Taurus sun), whose relating phrase is "pleasingly producing."

In the case of our friend Mr. Pitt, we look up his signs (moon in Capricorn, sun in Sagittarius) and find that he is "constructively seeking."

Moon Sign	Keyword	Keyword	Sun Sign
Aries	Actively	Asserting	Aries
Taurus	Steadily	Producing	Taurus
Gemini	Swiftly	Communicating	Gemini
Cancer	Carefully	Nurturing	Cancer
Leo	Dramatically	Expressing	Leo
Virgo	Accurately	Perfecting	Virgo
Libra	Pleasingly	Harmonizing	Libra
Scorpio	Intensely	Engaging	Scorpio
Sagittarius	Adventurously	Seeking	Sagittarius
Capricorn	Constructively	Ordering	Capricorn
Aquarius	Idealistically	Aspiring	Aquarius
Pisces	Sensitively	Inspiring	Pisces

Next, select the two cards that represent the sun and moon signs of your romantic partner, colleague, friend, or other person in whom you are interested. We'll repeat the same process for Brad's partner, Angelina Jolie. She has moon in Aries and sun in Gemini, so her two cards are the Emperor and the Lovers, with the phrase "actively communicating."

We then lay out the cards in the centre of our reading table:

Brad   Angelina

Marrying Cards: Brad Pitt and Angelina Jolie (The Universal Tarot)

Shuffle the rest of the deck, asking, "How do **Constructively Seeking** and **Actively Communicating** marry together?"

Select out seven cards and lay them out around the marrying cards as in the diagram following. If you require even more detail, pull an additional two cards.

Marriage Cards Spread (The Universal Tarot)

The positions (with 8 and 9 being optional for intermediate or advanced readers) signify:

1. What person 1 will look to achieve from the relationship.
2. What person 2 will look to achieve from the relationship.
3. What resources person 1 will want to express in the relationship.
4. What resources person 2 will want to express in the relationship.
5. The past that person 1 will need to clear in the relationship.
6. The past that person 2 will need to clear in the relationship.
7. The most harmonious marriage possible for these two people.

Optional additional cards

8. What can be developed out of and beyond the relationship.

9. What the relationship requires for fuel.

You can then compare and contrast the pairs of cards to interpret how these solar and lunar forces will play out within the relationship. This is a very comprehensive method of examining the inner and outer dynamics of a relationship as an expression of our inner self.

The Broken Relationship Game

In this method, we will play a game in a group to explore how the cards tell us about problems in relationships. As we've said, this is the most common theme you will be asked about as a reader; three out of five questions are about relationships. This game is played in a group of three. Choose two players to be "in relationship." The other player will be the "breaker." You can rotate your places after you have played the game once, so everyone has a turn as "breaker."

Take out the court cards from your deck. Shuffle them and allow the two people "in relationship" to select one card each. These are displayed face-up on the table, so all can see which court card each of them is embodying.

Shuffle the remainder of the deck. The "breaker" selects one card, hidden from the other players.

Each turn of the game now works like so:

1. Player 1 "in relationship" makes a statement about the relationship in the context or character of their court card. For example, if they had the King of Swords, they might say, "How about we decide once and for all where we are going out tonight?"

2. Player 2 "in relationship" responds likewise, in the character
of or inspired by their court card. For instance, if they had

the Page of Wands, they might reply, "Well, I thought I might just go for a walk by myself."

3. The "breaker" player now takes a turn. Inspired by his chosen card (which remains hidden), he says something to one or both of the other players designed to "break" the relationship. So if he had the Three of Cups, for example, he might say to Player 2, "You do realise he (the King of Swords) is partying behind your back?"

4. At this point, both players "in relationship" can make a guess at which card the "breaker" holds. The aim of the game is for the players "in relationship" to discern the exact card that the "breaker" holds before their relationship is totally broken. Once this is done to your satisfaction, you can rotate places, shuffle the deck again, and choose different cards.

5. If the "breaker" card cannot yet be guessed correctly, Player 1 must make a further statement about the relationship, either ignoring or taking on board what the "breaker" has said. Player 2 can respond, and then the "breaker" can have another turn at somehow sowing discord, disharmony, lack of mutual trust, derision, guilt, and so on, as his particular card dictates, into the narrative or conversation between the cards/characters in relationship.

This game is designed to encourage participants to see how cards can function in (and out of) relationship questions.

Loves Me/Loves Me Not Method

This method uses the whole deck, magically dividing it three times to arrive at an eight-card spread (or, optionally, a sixteen-card spread for more advanced readers). It also uses the magical terms of alchemy, with a little twist to produce a special "altar card" for midsummer enchantment. If performed at this time of year, the magic is strong, and even the performing of this spread may weave its own subtle changes.

Take the entire deck and shuffle whilst considering a relationship you'd like to know more about. Place it face-down and take the bottom card, which is the "base card." This indicates the real basis on which the relationship is founded.

Take the remaining deck and deal it alternately into two piles, face-down, saying "loves me" and "loves me not" as you lay down each card. The "loves me" pile is the first, to your left, and "loves me not" is the pile to the right.

You will have one card remaining in your hand. This is your special summer solstice altar card and should be placed on top of the base card. This indicates the enchantment required in your relationship at this time. It could also indicate a need to break an enchantment!

Next, discard the "loves me not" pile and pick up the "loves me" pile. Deal the cards into two new piles, left and right, saying "loves me" and "loves me not" as before.

Discard the "loves me not" pile and repeat again for a third time (third time's the charm!) with the "loves me" pile. You should now have two piles of nine cards each in the "loves me" and "loves me not" positions and one card remaining in your hand.

Place this final card face-down until you have read the two piles. This is your result card for the question "loves me or loves me not?"

We now read the "loves me" pile by turning the cards face-up and reading them one at a time according to the interpretation below. You can also read them as a simple story or purely intuitively.

We have used alchemical terms since alchemy is all about transformation. The cards indicate the ways in which you can transform your relationship.

You can read the "loves me" pile as follows:

1. Calcination: This first card is all about the pacing of the passion. The card in this position indicates whether you

need to change the tempo of your relationship. In other words, are things moving too fast, or not fast enough?

2. Solution: How can the waters of love heal any hurt in this relationship?

3. Coagulation: What most holds us together?

4. Sublimation: How can I go beyond the ploys and plays in this relationship? On what part of the game in this relationship am I most dependent? What needs releasing?

5. Mortification: What must be destroyed and transformed?

6. Separation: What is my own role in this and all my relationships?

7. Conjunction: What can I embrace to be true to my instincts?

8. Projection: What is the gift I bring to others through this relationship?

9. Summary: What are the positive qualities of this relationship?

You can also read the "loves me not" pile as follows, comparing the cards in the same positions in both piles.

1. Calcination: What spark is burning out in this relationship?

2. Solution: What is slowly dissolving in this relationship?

3. Coagulation: In what way does my fear of rejection play out in this relationship?

4. Sublimation: How can I elevate this relationship to a more spiritual level?

5. Mortification: What deadens this relationship? Where is the lead that must be turned to gold?

6. Separation: What is the role of the other person in this relationship?

7. Conjunction: How do I come together on the physical level with the other person?

8. Projection: What does the other person project onto me?

9. Summary: What are the negative qualities of this relationship?

You can now turn up that result card and get a final answer to your question, in the light of all you have read!

This method can be extremely powerful at uncovering points of transformation within a relationship at any stage. It is a wonderful reading to do at the summer solstice as the light shines so brightly upon all relationships, offering nurturing, healing, and openness to change. And if your reading is somewhat more challenging than you might want…

"If we shadows have offended,
Think but this, and all is mended,
That you have but slumber'd here
While these visions did appear.
And this weak and idle theme,
No more yielding but a dream…"[26]

Ripple Spreads

As we discussed briefly in chapter 2, ripple spreads show the ramifications of a particular choice or choices and how those choices are interconnected with each other. Too many "flat spreads" (of which there are way too many to name and number) are disjointed examinations of a situation from a number of different aspects—past, present, and future, for example—without offering real depth.

In a ripple spread, we lay out the cards as a sequence of "wave fronts" emerging from one or a number of events, whether they be past, present, future, possible, historical, and so on. Some ripple spreads work with the way ideas in the mind generate closed loops, leading to apparently insurmountable situations and dilemmas in life. A ripple spread can break through that by incorporating the reality of the loop in the layout.

Between Two Stools (A Ripple Spread)

This spread is most useful for assisting someone to divine a route between two difficult situations (or people!)—in other words, a "between the devil and the deep blue sea" type situation.

The question should clearly reference both situations or choices: "I am looking at either leaving my husband for my boyfriend, or staying put and breaking it off with my boyfriend" or "I have two houses I can move into, but am unsure which one." Choose two significators, one for each person or situation. Place them apart from each other.

Say, "This is the first ripple from situation 1" and lay out two cards as if they were ripples from the significator for situation 1. Read the two cards.

Say, "This is the first ripple from situation 2" and lay out two cards. Read the two cards.

Then do the same with three cards for each situation. Note any major differences, similarities, symbols, and so on as you divine the impact of both situations. It may become clear quite quickly which one is most likely or desirable.

Where the ripples merge on the table, you can draw cards to show the interference—the likely impact of not doing anything, or the situation as it presently exists. These "emerging cards" can also be read as the best possible outcome.

In this spread we can look at how future events are impacting the present, rather than the other way around. You can use any number of cards for this type of spread and arrange them as you wish. As an intermediate spread, it is dependent on your skill and intuition as you lay them out. The cards will guide you if you let them.

The Gates of Valentine (A Gated Spread)

This method of using tarot is completely unique and applies to relationships, whether with a loved one, partner, husband or wife, family member, close friend, working colleague, or even relationships in general. It requires up to a week of participation, with a simple drawing of cards taking less than ten minutes each day. The aim of the exercise is to explore, develop, and change through action our relationship(s). We hope you will find this revolutionary method useful to you in your personal life, as well as a method to teach your own students, friends who are tarot readers, or clients with whom you use tarot.

Whilst some decks are better than others for this particular spread, your personal choice is paramount, although we would not recommend any particularly esoteric deck. A Waite-Smith deck or clone, or a deck geared to relationships, such as Jane Lyle's Lovers Tarot, is ideal.

The days ahead will be challenging, intriguing, totally original, and magical. We hope that this activity provides your relationship with new insight, development, and change—and gives you a whole new way of looking at tarot.

Gate 1: Ticket to the Tunnel of Love

As discussed earlier, gated spreads are designed to a fundamental archetypal pattern and are linked together in a series so that each spread depends on the one before it. Not only that, but each spread requires an action in real life before progressing to the next spread. In this way, a spread may not make sense unless you have accomplished the tasks of the previous gates.

Our theme of relationships for this particular journey takes us to the Tunnel of Love, where our first task is to buy a ticket.

To perform the first gate, we select out all forty of the minor arcana cards. Shuffle them and select one card; this is your ticket card.

The ticket card depicts a requirement to manifest something—to pay in some way for your ticket—thus it requires you to do some activity within the following twenty-four hours. As an example, we'll use the Five of Wands. In the Tarot of Dreams, this card shows five masculine figures wielding staves in combat against a fiery background. This might indicate that tomorrow you'll need to fight for something in your relationship(s)—perhaps more than once.

Not only must you act upon this card as a general theme, but a gated spread also requires you to actually perform a deliberate act that you would not have done otherwise, which can be immediately attributed to your chosen card. So you might, for example, make a telephone call, speak to a particular person, or send a document that you would not have done otherwise. This is directly associated with the nature of the Five of Wands being combative or stressful.

Gate 2: Twists and Turns in the Tunnel of Love

We like to turn tarot into a very active, dynamic, oracular experience that causes you to relate to the cards in a new way. This also helps you read the cards from deep personal experience; you will have truly lived the tarot in real life.

This next gate lasts for three days before taking us to the final gate of Valentine. At that point we will reveal who our "favourite miss" is and how we will "steal a kiss" from her!

Here we do something different: take out all the cups, ace to ten. Lay these out face-up in a column, in order. Then shuffle the remaining cards in the deck whilst contemplating the twists and turns of relationships and looking up and down the column of cups.

When you are ready, stop shuffling and lay out one card from the deck next to each of the cup cards, starting with the ace and ending with the ten. You should have two columns, with the cups in order on one side, and on the other a card from the shuffled deck, paired with each cups card.

These ten pairs represent the twists and turns of the tunnel of love. In every cup card is depicted an aspect of our emotional life and relationship to the Universe (and others). They also depict our internal self-relationship and the unconscious contracts we create between all the aspects of our self.

The card we have taken from the shuffled deck is the divination for how we are best advised to approach these aspects—our attitude or angle. So for all ten aspects of our emotional life in relationship, we are given a card that depicts the current engagement of that aspect in the rest of our life. Over the next three days, feel free to explore this spread, discuss it on the Tarot-Town.com forum, and if it prompts actions, *take them*. Here are some keywords and key phrases to assist in your navigation of the tunnel:

Cups in Relationship

1. Arousal: What is it that excites you without pause?
2. Proximity: To whom can you can get physically close?
3. Similarity: Whom are you like, and whom do you like to be around?
4. Forgiveness: How do you show kindness and appreciation?
5. Inhibition: What holds you back?
6. Touch: What makes you feel truly in touch with the world and yourself?
7. Novelty: When was the last time you did something extraordinary?
8. Vulnerability: Do you remove yourself and avoid relationship?
9. Disclosure: What secrets do you keep, and how open can you be?
10. Commitment: What do you honour and value, and how do make your oaths?

So for example, if you pulled the Emperor against the Ace of Cups, you might see that you need to be more dynamic about going with what excites you—in other words, feeling the fear and doing it anyway! If you then pulled the Page of Wands against the next Cups card, the two, you might be looking to go on a journey to get close to someone—perhaps a friend. If you next pulled the Seven of Swords against the Three of Cups, that might be warning of a twist in the tunnel, where someone or something could take away your ability to be around similar people. And so on for all ten Cups.

This exercise is designed to be thought-provoking and to provide full navigation of the twists and turns of the tunnel! As you can see, what we have done here is to focus on one area of our lives (our emotions) through the map of tarot and measure everything else against that sequence.

Gate 3: Steal a Kiss from Your Favorite Miss

This is the third and finishing gate of our Valentine's experience. Here we reveal that our "favorite miss" is our very own soul—in other words, our soul in relationship to the Universe itself. This engagement between ourselves and the Universe is the most personal, intimate presence we hold.

It is indeed our Favorite Miss, and has been known in mysticism and magic as Shekinah, Gnosis, and Sophia—all feminine expressions of the divine dwelling in the real world. It is the true mystery of love and relationship: our very own heart open to the Universe. As Crowley wrote, "I am divided for love's sake, for the chance of Union."

So having dwelt this week upon our relationships with others and ourselves, we come now to the relationship of our soul to the divine. If we have travelled our gates honestly and with courage, we will have nothing to fear from the answer, which now awaits our kiss.

To perform this final gate—a true divination, simple yet profound—spend a few moments by yourself, for this is a personal reading of the highest order.

Then shuffle your deck and lay out four cards in the shape of a kiss (x):

Receiving   Unified By

Expressing   Divided By

These cards are a kiss from Sophia—Wisdom herself—accessed by your journey through the gates of the tunnel of love. They tell you truly:

Receiving: What gift the Universe has for you in love.

Unified By: How you can relate to the Universe spiritually.

Expressing: What gift you can bring to the Universe in love.

Divided By: How you avoid relationship and how to transcend that issue.

———

We look forward to hearing, if you will share in Tarot-Town.com, what Sophia has to tell you. We trust that Valentine's Day (or whenever you choose to perform this gated spread) will always be a reminder of the place of love in relationship, within the spiritual context of your life.

Eight

Facing Yourself:
Tarot for
Self-Discovery

During the 1990s, Marcus experimented with a method called the Inner Guide Meditation, from the book of the same name by the late Edwin Steinbrecher. In this method of inner exploration, tarot cards are used to create an illustration of a personal birth chart, allowing one to work with the tarot as a powerful and personalised self-change method. As a development of Steinbrecher's original system, Marcus added the esoteric technique of using "coded questions." These are used by another person to question a person's inner guide in such a manner that the person being asked—or, technically, their visualised inner guide or visualised tarot archetypes—could not know what was being asked of them.[27]

An example would be asking the meditating person—who is visualising a scene, perhaps, where he is standing with his inner guide and a representation of the High Priestess card—the question, "Ask the High Priestess: M. D. N?"

The person might reply, "The High Priestess is giving me a silver coin and telling me—this is odd—to bury it, by the fence outside the house."

Unknown to him is that the question was a coded version of "How should Marcus deal with his noisy neighbours?" This was an issue Marcus (as an example) had raised some weeks prior in another context, and the questioner thought it would make a good test, since Marcus would not have expected him to be asking that question.

When Marcus went and buried a silver coin by the fence, the neighbours suddenly moved out within the following week.

The moral of this story is that inner exploration with the tarot is the same as outer. The cards do not know they are only in our imagination.

In this chapter, we will explore various ways in which tarot can be used to map out the landscape of our own self. We'll look at dream work with tarot, and we'll use a helpful spread to reach a personal goal. We'll also take a ride on a "ghost train" in a gated spread. In this latter exercise, we will connect to our own history, using tarot to illuminate our past as well as our future. Few people come to a tarot reading to ask the question, "What was going on when X happened to me a few years ago?" However, the cards can discover the very patterns that created the present, empowering the individual to create a more fulfilling future.

The Nature of Unconscious Communication

The tarot creates a living landscape, with innumerable variations, of metaphors and symbols. This landscape may be populated by unicorns and faeries, or by dark figures and living statues. It may resemble medieval Europe, a Victorian city, or an alien world. It may even be the recognisable streets of present-day New York City or London.

In this sense, the tarot is similar to a dreamscape—a window into whatever lies beneath and beyond the symbols, a message given through metaphor. We must be aware of how this dreamscape works, for it is a tricky place where time can flow backward as well as forward, characters can change appearance on a whim, and literally anything can happen.

When you examine your dreams or visualisations, keep an eye out for any of the following. You can see how many of these also apply to tarot.

- Visual puns ("running around")
- Literal puns ("beside yourself")
- Ambiguous words ("spirit," "matter")
- Body language puns ("heartbroken," "a pain in the neck")

The Garden Walk

For this exercise, you'll get best results from using a deck that is either your most favourite or least favourite; using one you are not particularly interested in will be less provocative and engaging.

Shuffle the cards whilst thinking of all the times in your life when you have felt creative, imaginative, and playful.

When you're ready, take the top ten cards from the deck, turn them face-up, and throw them to the floor or onto the table! Spread them out a little; they should be slightly scattered.

Turn the rest of the deck upside-down to reveal the base card, and place that somewhere suitable to act as the "garden gate" into the spread.

Next, we simply go for a metaphorical Tarot Walk to discern the relationship between the various cards. You can choose any route at all, starting from the gate card and meandering through the other cards in whatever order you like. Sketch out the route you take in your journal, and stop when you feel you have exited the garden through another card.

For example, we walked from the Star gate to the Empress, the Two of Wands, the Five of Pentacles, and then exited with the Magician. We therefore read these five cards as a 5-card walk through our 10-card garden. We can take any route we wish. Number these routes (it is best to have at least three connections) and write down the connecting cards. In this example:

1. The Star: The Empress
2. The Empress: Two of Wands
3. Two of Wands: Five of Pentacles
4. Five of Pentacles: The Magician

Now write a brief impression of the nature of the route or connection between each pair of cards. This should take into account everything you know about the cards, such as Kabbalistic or numerological associations, astrological correspondences, keywords, your intuitive impressions... anything.

So, for example, we might write:

1. Falling from the heavens. Sky to earth. The drop.
2. Son sets sail, leaving home.
3. Hard times from hopeful beginnings.
4. A mentor teaches those who come inside. Choices.

Repeat this path-walking to discover other connecting paths in the garden. See which cards always seem to lend the same meaning to their connecting paths, and which cards appear to mean very different things when connected with different cards. Most importantly, see what themes emerge in common across any or all of the paths.

The Ghost Train (A Gated Spread)

In this next activity, we'll use another gated spread to connect with our ancestors. Whilst it can be performed at any time, it is particularly attuned to the week that ends on Hallowe'en or Samhain night.[28]

This is a personal spread, and you need not share any of what follows unless you find it supportive and helpful to do so. Our gated spread experiences often go deeper than we might imagine, so please hold tightly onto the handles at all times.

Gate 1: Carriage Card

Select out the major arcana cards from the deck and shuffle them. Consider all that has carried you through life, what you have clung to when things have been bad. Choose a card and look at it. This is your Carriage Card. What does it mean to you in terms of resources to carry you through a difficult or challenging time? How does the energy or lesson(s) pictured by your Carriage Card assist you in your life? Allow a day to pass whilst you consider this, and don't forget to write about it in your journal.

Gate 2: Sepia Photographs

At the next gate, the carriage starts up and we enter into the darkness... the lights dim, the train clatters and clanks, and we are soon engulfed by the acrid smell of smoke and dust. Then we turn a corner and to our left an eerie scene unfolds, sepia-coloured: an old Victorian parlour, with photographs on a mantelpiece and a piano. All of a sudden, the piano starts to play a haunting tune, and the photographs come to life, all speaking in whispers. They have something to tell us, if only we can hear them...

Firstly, you will need to list the names of a number of your ancestors (ten at most). These are family members who are no longer with you. If you can, find a photograph of each. If not, simply use a small card or piece of paper with each name written upon it. Take a day to locate photos or make named cards; you can also use old letters, jewelry, or other objects that connect you to those ancestors. If you do not know of any family ancestors, you can simply write "Father," "Grandmother," and so on. Lay out the photos and objects where they won't be disturbed.

To complete Gate 2, remove all the court cards from your deck and place at least one next to each of the photographs or name cards. Select them based on your intuition; allow your hands to automatically draw certain cards together with their appropriate ancestor. Open yourself entirely to the process.

When you feel like you're done, leave the cards and photos spread out. You'll return to them tomorrow.

Gate 3: Spooky Pipe Organ Music

The next day, as the carriage rounds another bend, and with the memory of those photographs still in our hearts and minds, we see a ghastly organist playing an ancient pipe organ, with discordant sounds echoing in the dark as we plummet farther into the tunnels of the Ghost Train.

Take your tarot deck, minus your Carriage Card and the court cards, and shuffle it. Now go through it and select out the cards that, to you, seem to embody the darker side of life—the mistakes, regrets, and fears in the night. These are the notes of the pipe organ, echoing discordantly in our lives.

Whether you've chosen one card or many, fan them out in front of the layout of your court cards and ancestor items.

In our next gate, we will start to really see how a gated spread works, with our first real-world activity bridging two gates.

Gate 4: The Planchette

With the shivers from the spooky pipe organ music still running down our spines, the Ghost Train picks up speed and careens around the next dark turn. We can hear the shrieks and gasps of our companions as the train hurls us into the darkness. Then suddenly we emerge into a huge space, dimly lit, full of cobwebs brushing on our faces and candles burning. In the centre, we see a table surrounded by Victorian women and men—we can tell this from their clothes, at least, as their bodies have long since turned into skeletons.

They are holding a séance, and we see that above them hovers a spectral presence—a ghost of times past, an ancient voice, a call to our own ancestors. It is pointing at us, asking us something, demanding something... but what?

Take your Carriage Card and place your finger on it.

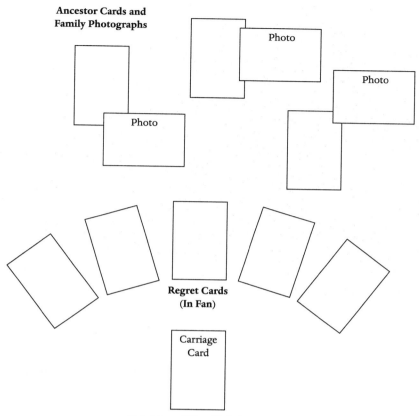

Ancestor Cards and
Family Photographs

Photo

Photo

Photo

Regret Cards
(In Fan)

Carriage
Card

Gated Spread Ghost Train Layout

Sliding it around like a planchette, allow it to move so it points to any or all of your "regrets and mistakes" cards. Gaze at your ancestor cards. Allow the Carriage Card to stop when it is pointing to the "regrets and mistakes" card that seems most powerful to you at this time.

Now consider together the Carriage Card, the "regrets and mistakes" card, and the ancestor card(s) you were gazing at when the Carriage Card stopped.

Consider what this combination of cards is asking you to do now in your life, before Hallowe'en is upon us. How can the Carriage Card carry you through resolving the negativity shown by the "regrets and mistakes" card? How does that relate to your ancestry? Perhaps it may simply be a case of sitting down for five minutes and remembering good times and honouring a memory. Perhaps you need to write an e-mail or a letter, or go see someone. Perhaps you need to do something to celebrate your living family members, or something entirely unexpected. Let the cards (and the ancestors) talk to you.

Here we'd like to give you an example. When Marcus last performed this gated spread, his Carriage Card was the Devil. In Gate 4, it pointed to the "regrets and mistakes" card of the Tower. He was looking at a group of his ancestors, seven sons/brothers, when the Carriage Card stopped, so it indicated not one particular ancestor, but all of them together.

He took this to signify that his real-life activity that day would be to hold tight to his direction (the Devil) and do something dramatic and instant (the Tower). However, the day turned out to be full of emotional shocks (the Tower), against which the best course of action was to keep true to himself (the Devil). He really felt the Ghost Train during the day, with lots of Tower-like events threatening to derail him. He felt lucky that he saw it this way round; otherwise he might have done something in reaction, which would not have been the best way to handle things.

What has this to do with the ancestors? Well, here's the weird thing. He was explaining this to someone and said, "I guess it's like some sort of fairground ride, holding onto the handles tight whilst there's all hell breaking loose around you—especially as the apparent chaos and danger is not real." Then he went on to say, out of the blue, "Perhaps it's what those men felt in the Great War, just holding tight to whatever they could to get through it, whilst the horrors unfolded about them."

All of a sudden all the hairs went up on the back of Marcus's neck as he felt an instant emotional connection and sense of respect for the bravery of those men, his ancestors. It was a visceral surge, and very profound. He realised that he should learn to honour and respect the sacrifices they made by ensuring that he lives his life to the fullest, in whatever way he chooses, since some of his own ancestors did not get such a choice. It helped him see a little deeper into the world and gain a better viewpoint on his own problems.

This is what a gated spread is all about: engaging with life on deeper levels and in profound ways, which we may not have done otherwise. If you are doing this exercise in the week before Samhain, the final gate should take place on Samhain night itself. It will require that you have completed the activity from Gate 4. The purpose and uniqueness of gated spreads is that they are interwoven with real-life activities.

Gate 5: Emerging Whole

Here we arrive at our final gate in the Ghost Train, on Hallowe'en night itself, the end of the Celtic year, the time when the veil between worlds is thin, and nature itself begins the descent into healing darkness.

On our train, we emerge through a forest scene, a long path with trees closing in on each side. In those wilds we see dark shapes, moving shadows, bats flitting, red eyes balefully glaring—primitive horrors and dangers interwoven with the webs of spiders.

But we hold on fast, because ahead of us we see a door opening, the end of the ride. We know our friends and family, those who haven't taken this ride, are waiting for us beyond it. Take the rest of the deck (from which we have taken out the Carriage Card, the court cards, and the "regret and mistake" cards) and shuffle it whilst considering your family, friends, colleagues, and coworkers. Also consider the future, and the children of whom you are or will be an ancestor.

Consider particularly the action you took at the previous gate. You are in a place in life where you can do things, where you can affect the outcomes of the world. What did you do to respond to the voices of the past? What can you do?

Now take three cards from the deck without looking, and lay them out, face-up, in front of the Carriage Card (see Gated Spread Ghost Train Layout). These are the "legacy" cards, showing your inheritance, your present situation, and your legacy that you leave to those who follow you.

With those lessons in mind, connecting all the past with all the future, we ride our carriage into the light, beyond our most primitive fears, to a place where we may someday come face to face with our ancestors.

The Miracle Card Method

This method is taken from solution-oriented therapy methods, where all self-discovery is utilised to access resources leading directly to a stated solution. In effect, it is as if in a tarot reading we determine the outcome card for ourselves, and then the reading is done to demonstrate how we reach that self-selected outcome.

It is particularly useful as a method for those already reasonably sure in their life choices and path, but who require additional insight to reach an already determined goal or to resolve a difficult situation. While it is demonstrated here as a reading for oneself, it can also be an effective tool for quick readings, as in a social setting.

Select out the sixteen court cards and go through them, face-up. Choose one to indicate who you would be on the other side of your problem or after you've reached your goal.

Here are some questions to consider as you make your choice: "What would it be like, and feel like, if you waved a miracle wand and your issue was resolved? How would you know? What would be happening in your life? Which of these cards illustrates that the most?"

Next, select out all the minor cards and go through them, face-up. Choose one to show the external situation on the other side of the problem—the solution reached, or the goal achieved. This could be, for example, the Ten of Cups, showing a contented domestic situation, or the Ace of Pentacles, showing a new business opportunity.

Next, select out all the major cards and go through them, face-up. Choose one for the "miracle card" that would get you to that chosen destination, as the person you chose from the court cards. Lay out these three cards in a row.

Now put the remaining cards back together in one single pile, and shuffle whilst considering your desired outcome card, your resulting state card, and your miracle card.

When you feel ready, take the top three cards and lay them, face-up, on top of the three already selected cards. This three-card reading shows exactly how you can reach the goal or solve the problem.

The miracle card, we always say, is in a person's hands—the trick is discovering how to open our hands to receive it, which is what the three drawn cards will illustrate.

Tarot in Your Sleep

In this section, we present a few ways by which you can incorporate your tarot learning into dream work. In the ancient Greek oracular tradition at Delphi, this was called *Eghimiseos*. It was said that if you slept at the site of a particular shrine, the god of that shrine would present you an oracle in your sleep. In the exercises that follow, you will see how to encourage these oracular visitations. As with many of the methods in this book, you will build up to the full experience by practising skills first, then the method that uses these skills.

Dream-walking the Suits

Our first exercise is simply to practice the skill of visualisation. As we discussed previously, this is not just to say that we see things inside our head; our representation of the external world can also be composed of sounds, feelings, scents, even tastes. Which tarot card embodies the taste of success? And when you have tasted that card, what does success taste like? Can you hear the pipes in the Six of Pentacles, the tumble of the coins in the water, and can you taste the water in the air? What about the rich scent of the fruit in the Seven of Pentacles, and the touch of morning dew on your face as you look at the delicate web in the Eight? As we approach the Nine of Pentacles, what music fills the glade? In which card in the Waite-Smith deck can we smell a rat, even if one is not illustrated?

6, 7, 8, 9 of Pentacles (Shadowscapes Tarot)

With these sensory impressions in mind, take your tarot deck and choose any one of the suits. If you choose to do them in a Kabbalistic order, follow this sequence: Pentacles, Swords, Cups, and Wands.

Pull out the numbered cards in that suit from ace to ten. Take a good look at them, and place them in a pile beside your bed.

As you go to sleep, visualise the ace of the suit. What details can you recall? Don't refer back to the card; keep your eyes closed. If all you see is a general blur of the "ace-ishness" of the "Pentacles-thingy," that's fine. Step into that detail, or peer through it, no matter how undefined it is. Then start to sense the two of the suit. This may bring to mind immediately some particular detail of the card, perhaps a ship in the distance. That's great.

Now see whatever else you can recall about the card—the detail, the colours, the artwork—along with any other impressions of feeling, touch, scent, or taste.

Then move on to the next card in sequence. The aim is to be able to walk through the entire suit, in crisp clear detail, with every card fixed in your mind. This is an exercise Marcus did for over eight months when he was first learning tarot, when he was fifteen—although he says he still gets the Sixes and Sevens of Swords confused sometimes!

When you have mastered all four suits, you can try walking through the entire fifty-six cards of the minor arcana in sequence. This is something Tali found very useful when undergoing a routine CAT scan recently; it ensured that her mind was occupied with something far more engaging than the clunking of magnets and machinery in an enclosed space for an hour. And although many of us are more or less familiar with the imagery of the major arcana, you will benefit by doing this exercise with them, too.

Lucid Dreaming the Cards

If you use tarot regularly, you may find that you dream entire spreads. These can appear not just as abstract imagery—"I dreamt of a boat, just like the boat on the Six of Swords"—but as actual readings or combinations of cards that are significant in some way.

One dream recently had Marcus on a pirate ship, along with comedians performing a Shakespearean play. This was probably because he had been discussing the Pirate Tarot and the William Blake Tarot decks the night previously. Within the dream, he was handed a wooden tray in which were slots, and pegged into those slots were wooden blocks, each painted on four sides with one tarot image. The four images were the Moon, the Hermit, the Six of Wands, and the Four of Wands, from the Druidcraft Tarot deck. These had direct relevance to an upcoming trip the following week, and the fact that they were to do with travel was illustrated by the pirate ship.

In order to encourage lucid dreaming, here are several of our favourite techniques.

Hand Observation

As you get ready for bed, for about thirty minutes prior, watch your hands carefully. This may be whilst you are washing or folding clothes, tidying up, or other tasks. You may watch your hands closely whilst you have a drink or eat. Pay particular attention to your hands as often as possible—which is not something you will usually find yourself doing at any other time.

You may not notice anything for a few nights; however, if you maintain this practice, you should find yourself suddenly coming awake a few times during the night, every few nights. (Of course, do not continue the practice if you have difficulty getting back to sleep or if it impacts your waking life.) What is happening is that you are noticing your hands in your dream, and because you have also been doing so with your conscious attention, it anchors you to that conscious, attentive, waking state. This usually brings you briefly and sharply to sudden wakefulness.

After about a week, start to "gently" observe your hands. This is a hard state to describe; however, imagine that your mind is dancing in harmony with your hands as you observe them before bed. There is a soft and gentle flow of activity, ceaseless and continual, and all is well. There is no particular beginning or end, there is no aim in mind, just the constant presence of your hands and your awareness of your connection to them.

After a couple of days (or maybe longer) of this observation, you may find yourself coming to lucid attention within your sleep, without waking up! This is a curious state, and it is possible that the first time you experience it, you will be so amazed that you wake right up in surprise. Return to the gentle flow of your hand observation, and after a little bit more practice you will be able to maintain the lucid dream state for quite some time.

Constant Enquiry

A second useful method is to constantly ask yourself, before and during your preparations for sleep? "Is this a dream or am I awake looking at (whatever you are looking at)" This can have the same results as the previous technique, and works for some who don't have success with that technique. There are many more methods for reaching the lucid dreaming state; have patience and experiment until you find the right one—it is worth it.[29]

Taking Your Cards into Your Dream

Once you have experienced a little bit of lucid dreaming, simply write the word "tarot" on the palm of your hand before sleep. Ensure that you write it in such a way that you can feel the marker pen on your hand; it must be a "felt" sensation that you can recall when asleep. You can also place a bangle around your wrist or a similar "feeling" item that you associate with tarot. It has to be something that prompts your body or your memory whilst you are asleep.

You can then continue your usual lucid dreaming practice, and add the "Dream-walking the Suits" method as you have already practised. Because you have now added a physical anchor to the idea of tarot, it is usually only a matter of a week or so until you will have your first tarot dream—and it may even be lucid, so you can engage and interact with the actual cards and figures.

It's an excellent idea to have a really good question to hand in case of any lucid encounter of a profound and powerful nature. We have known many students who worked very hard to gain this skill, mastered it, and then finally, after a year or two, had the Hierophant or the High Priestess show up in a lucid dream and proclaim, "What is it you ask of me?" only to have the student reply, "Oh, gosh, er … I'm not sure, I wasn't really expecting you."

Don't forget to keep a journal by your bed to record your dreams over this time, even if you don't remember them in detail. You can always write "no dreams recalled," or write about a vague sense of a semi-recalled dream—"Something about flowers or a garden, maybe. I felt a bit sad when I awoke but I think it was about the past…" Just making the effort to do so will help you learn to remember your dreams.

––––––––––

The tarot serves us as a pack of possibilities, a divination of the divine, a dynamic reflection of the psyche, a search engine of the soul, a GPS of the spiritual journey, and a mirror to our dreams. In coming face to face with the seventy-eight images of a tarot deck, we are coming face to face with ourselves. We may be surprised, then, to see in those very depths the same heights our soul seeks, reflected endlessly in a single universal face with seventy-eight diverse expressions.

Nine

Facing All Fronts:
Twelve Spreads

It is said that Dr. Milton Erickson, a famous psychiatrist and hypnotherapist, never repeated the same technique twice. He used two basic principles, incorporation and utilization, and from these everything else followed, naturally and instinctively. He simply incorporated into his method the actual communications of his clients—their language, nonverbal communication, and unconscious processes—and then utilized these exact same elements to effect massive change.

We saw earlier in this book how we can use a similar principle to generate elegant spreads based on the querent's own question. However, often students require a simple template—a spread—with which to practice. Unfortunately, because many students do not learn to go beyond this approach, they end up having to learn dozens of spreads, or else constantly ask, "What is the best spread for this question?" We decided to take all the questions asked of us over the last three decades, categorise them, and provide a set of twelve spreads that should cover the great majority of what is asked.

But know this—the most astonishing spread you will ever create is the one you will use only once, for one particular querent, for one particular question, in one particular moment.

The Truth of the Oracle must be discovered within the divinatory moment, not a template.

———————

Many spreads are available to frame a reading and provide a context within which interpretation can be carried out more precisely for the question being asked. Earlier, we provided a means of generating a spread straight from the question, and in this penultimate chapter we will show you twelve template spreads that can be used to answer the majority of questions you will encounter when reading for other people (or yourself). These spreads are based around an existing esoteric system that has already divided life into helpful sections—astrology with its twelve houses.

Twelve Spreads for the Whole of Life

The phrase "put your own house in order first" comes, as do many, from the Bible. In this case, from Isaiah (38:1):

In those days was Hezekiah sick unto death. And Isaiah the prophet the son of Amoz came unto him, and said unto him, "Thus saith the LORD, Set thine house in order: for thou shalt die, and not live."

We hope to set our house in order long before our appointed time by using tarot to explore the aspects of our life that require work and offer opportunities for development. We can also divine for questions posed by others in this same way.

In astrology, twelve specific areas of life correspond to twelve "houses" —divisions of the 360-degree birth chart into equal sections of 30 degrees each. Of course, there are many different house systems in astrology. The one utilised here is found in John Frawley's *The Real Astrology* and is based upon traditional horary astrology.[30] As Frawley points out—at length—

this system views some areas of the houses as being entirely malefic and troublesome, rather than through what he sees as a "modernist" gloss of positivity.

The twelve houses presented by Frawley use the Regiomontanus system of Johannes Müller von Königsberg (1436–1476), who used the pseudonym "King of the Mountains" (Regiomontanus) in his writings. However, the system had been in use long before his time.[31] The houses relate to the following aspects of earthly life:

1. "Spark" and your body
2. Resources and your inanimate and movable possessions
3. Siblings, neighbours, and communication
4. Land, property, security, your father
5. Children, pleasure, "ale-houses and taverns"
6. Service, ill health, and all that afflicts us
7. The other person, marriage, relationships
8. Death
9. God, religion, learning, dreams and visions
10. King, boss, your mother
11. Friends, friendship, hopes and wishes
12. Enemies, tribulation, sorrow

Each of these areas is very general, of course, but we can easily assign most questions to one of them. A question about a partner or potential partner—the most likely topic we are going to be asked about—is a seventh-house issue, although what we do with that person is a fifth-house issue!

A question about your career is possibly a tenth-house issue where it relates to a potential promotion, but is a ninth-house issue where it relates to improving your skills for that promotion. If the promotion is at present merely a vague wish or hope, then it falls into the eleventh house.

This is an important approach to looking into the very heart of a question posed to us in divination. As a contemporary oracle, we should always look into the context of the question to be assured that we are answering it in the world and environment in which it exists for the client, avoiding as much as possible interjecting our own beliefs and presumptions into the question. Although this is difficult in actual practice, we can limit our own projection by using a framework.

Whilst we could project our mundane life onto the stellar map and all twelve of its areas correspondence, we will benefit further by having a specific spread for each such area, appropriate to the nature of the question or situation.

Spread 1: The Soul Boat, for Matters of the House of the Self

Example questions: "Where is my life going?" "Who am I?" "What should I do?"

This spread is based on the ancient Egyptian concept of the "soul boat"—the barque of the sun. The sun was seen as traversing the sky in a vast boat, and the nature of the sun changed as the day progressed. As the central glyph of the self or soul, the Sun card is used here as the significator. The remaining cards are shuffled and dealt as depicted below. The ancient Egyptians also believed in a serpent adversary to the sun—Apep—which is reflected in the reading.

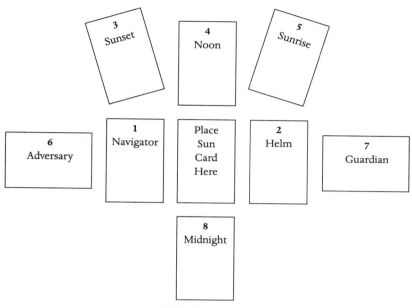

The Soul Boat Spread

1. Navigator: This card indicates what may be seen to steer you toward in your life journey, your vision and a signpost or beacon.

2. Helm: This illustrates your resources, things that can be drawn upon, avenues that can be explored, and assistance that can be given.

3. Sunset: This is a part of your life that must be allowed to fade.

4. Noon: This is a part of your life that must be recognised and enjoyed.

5. Sunrise: This is a part of your life that must be developed and nurtured.

6. Adversary: This is what blocks you.

7. Guardian: This is what defeats the blocks.

8. Midnight: This is the secret core of your life that must be brought into the light.

In this spread, you may wish to read the Helm and Guardian cards together and then the Adversary, for example, comparing it to the Midnight card. However, as with any other spread, do not mistake the positions and numbering as anything other than a convenient description—guidelines, if you will. You can read the cards in any order and recognise patterns as you do so. Listen to and trust your intuition.

Spread 2: The Well of Untapped Reserves, for Matters of the House of Resources

Example questions: "What am I missing?" "What do I need" "How can I make it happen?"

This unique spread utilises not only the symbol or image of a house—but actually your house or apartment itself! It is specifically designed as a reading for oneself. If performed on behalf of a client, you can do it as written, or map out (with the client) his or her house and use that as a layout. In Jungian terms, the house is a symbol of the self, and various locations in a house often appear in dreams to indicate aspects of the self. Here we also take the physical locations as representing functions.

Take your deck and shuffle, whilst standing in whatever place you regard as the centre of your home. Take out the first card and lay it somewhere in the space around you, saying: "This is the card that tells me exactly what I have."

Now move to the next room or area of your property, and lay out a card according to the function of that location. Here are some examples:

- Kitchen: "This is the card that tells what nourishes me."
- Study: "This is the card that tells what I can learn."
- Children's room: "This is the card that tells what delights me."
- Bedroom: "This is the card that tells what will give me rest and relaxation."

- Basement: "This is the card that tells what is hidden that I can draw upon."
- Attic: "This is the card that tells what I can aim for."
- Hallway: "This is the card that tells how I will get there."
- Bathroom: "This is the card that tells me what I must flush away."

Feel free to use your imagination in this reading and have fun with it. You can lay down more than one card in any particular area, if you like, and then go back through your property reading the cards. Be careful with this method not to lose any cards, though, or to perform the reading when there are lots of other people (or animals) passing through the place. Also take care not to get your cards wet or damp. Finally, whilst it is fun to go clambering into the attic to receive a message from the cards that otherwise would not make itself known, watch your step!

Spread 3: The Family and the Fishing Net, for Matters of the Family

Example questions: "How do I deal with my family (or a specific family member)?" "What's going to happen at the wedding?"

This is another example of using a split deck, as discussed earlier; in this case, the court cards are separated from the rest of the deck. It is also what we call a "layered spread" (as contrasted with a "flat spread")—in other words, it deals with situations that are still developing.

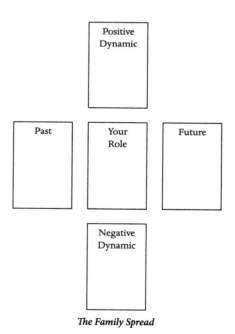

The Family Spread

Take out the sixteen court cards and shuffle them, thinking about the question. Lay them out in a cross as the diagram shows, starting from the top, then three cards left to right, and finally the fourth card at the bottom of the cross.

Set the rest of the court cards aside. Read these four cards first, then take the separated deck (composed of majors and minors only) and ask a related question, such as, "How can I mend relations with my sister?" Shuffle the deck and lay out one card on top of each of those already laid down. This will indicate the energy developing in that area of the situation. You can ask as many more questions as you wish, laying additional cards down on top of each stack.

Spread 4: The Tablet of Union, for Matters of Protection and Security

Example questions: "How can I best protect my job?" "How do I conclude a troubling matter?"

In the Enochian magical system developed by John Dee and Edward Kelley in the late sixteenth century, it was believed that the angels transmitted teachings of a vast and complex nature. At the centre of this system stood the Watchtowers of the Elements and an array of thirty *aethyrs,* which the angels inhabited and passed through, from one world into another.

To comprehend this vast system, a "Tablet of Union" was given, where a simple synthesis of the elements could be viewed and from which everything else followed. Here we take that elemental root to create a twenty-five-card spread that gives a comprehensive overview of a tricky situation.

	Spirit	Air	Water	Earth	Fire
Spirit	**1** Spirit of Spirit	**2** Spirit of Air	**3** Spirit of Water	**4** Spirit of Earth	**5** Spirit of Fire
Air	**6** Air of Spirit	**7** Air of Air	**8** Air of Water	**9** Air of Earth	**10** Air of Fire
Water	**11** Water of Spirit	**12** Water of Air	**13** Water of Water	**14** Water of Earth	**15** Water of Fire
Earth	**16** Earth of Spirit	**17** Earth of Air	**18** Earth of Water	**19** Earth of Earth	**20** Earth of Fire
Fire	**21** Fire of Spirit	**22** Fire of Air	**23** Fire of Water	**24** Fire of Earth	**25** Fire of Fire

Tablet of Union Spread

1. Where is this situation coming from, ultimately?
2. What is the simple idea that captures the heart of this event?
3. What is this situation trying to teach me?

4. How can I best bring it to conclusion safely?

5. Where can I best utilise my ambition (or passion) in this situation?

6. What needs communicating?

7. What is free to move?

8. How best can I maintain my emotional stability?

9. What must I see in order to understand the reality of this situation?

10. Where can I best spend my time?

11. Where am I safest?

12. Where can I discover clarity and expression?

13. What is free to be felt?

14. Where might I become unstuck?

15. Where is the source of tension and conflict?

16. What value needs to be drawn upon to protect those involved in this situation?

17. What is the simplest way of seeing what is going on?

18. What can I do about where I feel pinned down?

19. What is this situation trying to achieve in reality and manifestation?

20. What fire needs putting out immediately? What needs to be dealt with first?

21. What spark can I rescue from this situation?

22. What can I give life by paying attention?

23. How can I bring my own resources and feelings to bear in this situation?

24. What will assure long-term success and protection?

25. What is the ultimate message I must live?

Spread 5: The Self-Fulfilling Spread, for Matters of Pleasure and Joy

Example questions: "How can I improve my life?" "Where can I discover the joy of life?"

In this method for reading for oneself, you first select one card from the deck that best embodies your idea of a fulfilled and happy life. If you have more than one deck, you may wish to choose the one that has the most joyous images. You can also use this method with a querent by asking him or her to select such a card. Place that card on your table a short distance away from you.

Shuffle the rest of the deck whilst considering that card, and when you are ready, draw a card from the deck. Place that one directly in front of you. Say, "This is how it will go if I try to find joy."

If the card appears to be a negative one, or one that does not favor working toward your goal, say, "Okay, so I will go that way less." Set it aside and draw another.

If the card appears to fulfill a step toward your goal, say "Okay, so I will go that way more." Leave the card on the table.

Repeat the process until you have four or five cards that indicate the steps you must take to have pleasure and joy in your life.

If you need further clarification as to how to take action on each of those steps, we suggest you use the Next Step method included in both *Tarot Twist* and *Tarosophy*. Of course, you can also draw a further card for each step.

Spread 6: The Discover Your Demon Spread, for Matters of Affliction

Example questions: "Why do I always do that?" "Why am I depressed?" "Why is my life so negative?"

This method could be compared to an exorcism, to draw a demon out from hiding within a situation. The demon might be an attachment,

an old pattern, a self-destructive streak, or other negative re-
current situation. Whilst tarot
reading is not a replacement
for counselling or psychother-
apy, it does provide a means of
examining a personal situation
or behaviour with the intent of
gaining insight.

Consider the nature of the
affliction and lay out the first
four cards in order in the shape
of a cross as below.

These first four cards show:

Discover Your Demon Spread

1. The fear that is at work
   in this situation. The
   nature of what you are
   trying to avoid by playing out this pattern or by this pattern
   of events being present in your life.

2. The advice that can resolve (or even absolve) this situation,
   which you may not be ready to hear or act upon because
   you do not yet have the resources.

3. The resources or approach you can take to change this
   situation.

4. The actual first step of exorcising this behaviour or pattern
   of events from your life.

When you have considered these first four cards, take the rest of the deck and begin to shuffle the cards as violently as possible, contemplating the cross of cards before you. When you feel ready, say in a loud voice, "Demon begone!" and place the deck, face-down, in the centre of the cross.

Pause for a moment, then turn the deck face-up and look into the eyes of your demon, now identified and ready to be driven out.

Spread 7: The He Said, I Said Spread, for Matters of Relationship

Example questions: "What's going on in this relationship?" "Will this relationship last?"

The majority of questions asked of a tarot reader are about relationships. We've already discussed how prevalent these questions are and in how many ways they may be phrased. Here the cards will tell us about the nature of the communication between two people in a relationship, which will lead to a prediction of how the relationship may progress.

In this eight-card spread we use the four worlds of Kabbalah to view the relationship on all levels.

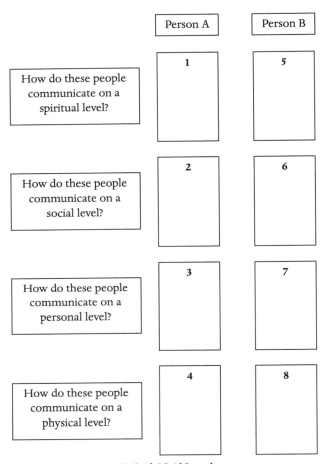

	Person A	Person B
How do these people communicate on a spiritual level?	1	5
How do these people communicate on a social level?	2	6
How do these people communicate on a personal level?	3	7
How do these people communicate on a physical level?	4	8

He Said, I Said Spread

In this spread we read as the diagram above, pairing the two cards on four different levels of the relationship. It can often be insightful to read each pair and then look at Partner A and B separately in the two rows.

Spread 8: The One Year to Live Spread, for Matters of Life and Death

Example questions: "What has my life held?" "How do I approach death?"

Begin this exercise with a moment's consideration of this scenario: you have been given an accurate prognosis of your death, in exactly one year from this moment. When you're ready, shuffle the deck and select twelve cards, one relating to each month to come and the main concern of that month. The cards can be laid out in a long line, in a grid of three cards by four cards, or in a large circle, whichever you prefer.

You can perform this spread as an exercise, or you can take these twelve cards as your "Contemplation Card of the Month" each month for the year to come. In this example, we have used the months January to December for convenience.

1. January: What is my initial reaction?
2. February: How do I prepare for death?
3. March: How do I live and heal?
4. April: How do I live each day?
5. May: How do I review my life?
6. June: How do I offer service?
7. July: Who dies?
8. August: What is beyond my death?
9. September: How do I leave my body and belongings?
10. October: What message do I leave behind?
11. November: What is change?
12. December: How do I die?

This is a profound reading and is worthy of your time to consider its results and write about them in your journal. You may wish to revisit this reading on occasion and add further notes over time.

This reading is unique in that the first time it is performed, it provides immediate answers for unlocking in your life. If you perform it again, it is never the same as the first reading—like hearing a joke for the second time or watching the same film again, knowing the surprise finale.

Spread 9: The Immanent Spread, for Matters of Spirit and Vision

Example questions: "What is the Universe about?" "Is there a God/dess?"

Although it would be nice to provide a spread that would give conclusive answers to such questions about the Universe and our role within it, this method merely allows the reader to practice experiencing the *immanence* of the world through tarot. It ties into the dream work we practiced in the last chapter, and is meant to be done over a period of three weeks.

To start, choose one major arcana card. Place it by your bed face-up and, for seven nights, visualise it before sleep in as much detail as you can. Record any dreams.

For the following seven nights, turn the card face-down and again visualise it in detail before sleep. Turn it up in the morning and, throughout the day, look for the card in your daily environment. As an example, if it were the Tower card, you might see a demolition of a chimney or a building on television or in real life. Make a note of the event.

For the next seven nights, visualise the whole universe existing inside that card, including yourself. Sense the presence of that card on the outer edge of everything that is occurring for the whole of that time. Make a note of any observations, experiences, and (particularly) coincidences.

You may find this exercise promotes intuitive awareness, strange events and experiences, and even synchronicities—visionary-type experiences of meaningful coincidence.

Spread 10: The Big Bad Boss Spread, for Matters of Career and Promotion

Example question: "Will I get that promotion?" "How do I progress in my career?"

The Big Bad Boss Spread works in a fixed and hierarchical fashion to replicate the conditions found in most workplaces and career paths. Ideally, it should be used in conjunction with such guidebooks as *What Colour is Your Parachute?* by Richard N. Bolles.

It's another example of using a split deck, and requires you to split the deck into three stacks: court cards, majors, and minors.

Take the court cards and select three—one for you, one for your current boss (or supervisor, or other person who has influence over you), and one for your desired position.

These are cards 1, 2, and 3.

Next, shuffle the minors and lay out two cards between the three court cards. These are your "resúmè cards" and indicate how you might progress from one position to the next. You can also add a major arcana card to the spread to divine what resources you can draw upon to make that step.

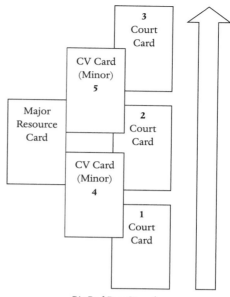

Big Bad Boss Spread

Spread 11: The Wish You Were Here Spread, for Matters of Hopes and Wishes

Example questions: "Will this outlandish project come to anything?" "Will a relationship develop between myself and X?"

When there is little history to determine whether a project, relationship, or creative venture will be successful, a tarot reading can divine the likely outcome based on a future-past perspective. In this spread, we look at the potential factors that lead to wishes being fulfilled. Since the eleventh house is particularly associated with friendship, we also look to see who can assist us in the fulfillment of these wishes and hopes.

Take the Star card, which we will use as a future significator, out of the deck. Place it in the centre of your table or reading space.

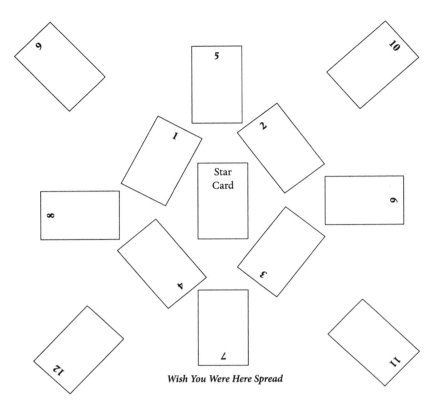

Wish You Were Here Spread

- Place a circle of four cards (1–4) around the Star card to divine the constraints of the situation.
- Place four "ray" cards (5–8) to show what can shine through those constraints.
- Place four "halo" cards (9–12) to show where help from others might be found.

Spread 12: The Brick Wall Spread, for Matters of Enmity and Sorrow

Example questions: "How do I overcome this state?" "How can I escape this situation?"

Our final spread in this chapter addresses the finality and "stuckness" of certain states, where we meet a dead end, a brick wall, or other metaphor for an apparently unchangeable situation. Here we'll divine a way to break through such states and situations by locating a "chink" in the wall, through which we can progress.

Shuffle the deck and, when you feel ready, lay down four cards to show the nature of the blockage in the stuck situation. Use your intuition and your assessment of the cards to discover where a "gap" might be found. This might be located between the cards with the largest numerical gap (for example, between an Ace of Wands and a Nine of Cups) or a gap in type (for instance, if three cards were minors and the fourth was a major). This will give a good indication of where leverage might be divined.

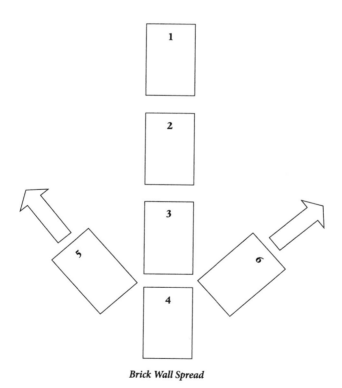

Brick Wall Spread

Next, lay out two cards to divine how that gap might be created, passed through, or exploited. You may wish to lay out further cards to show the steps required to do so.

With this range of spreads, you can confidently read for any of the central themes of human life. You should always be open to any question; our earlier chapters have shown you how to how to read for any question and how to turn any question into a spread. A gradual build-up of your skills combined with practice will soon have you reading tarot fearlessly and joyfully, looking forward to whatever new situations and learning opportunities may come your way.

Ten

Tarot in
the World

On May 25, 2010—World Tarot Day™—Tali and Marcus went into their local town square to conduct an experiment. They were acting as part of the world's largest tarot reading, which is conducted on that day each year, to divine the "spirit of tarot" for the year ahead. Local participants were challenged to perform at least seventy-eight one-card readings in one day. Their experiment was to see if they could simply walk up to people and offer them a free one-card reading. They videoed the entire day.[32]

The video shows about thirty scenes of Tali and Marcus approaching people politely and explaining their purpose. Without fail, each person showed exactly the same facial expressions in sequence as Tali and Marcus walked up to them:

1. *What's going on here?*

2. *Oh, I'll bet they're trying to sell me something.*

3. *They're not selling; it's some sort of charity thing.*

4. *It's not charity; it's some religious cult thing.*

5. *Oh no, it's not even that—it's TAROT!*

At that point, the video shows, time and time again, people almost literally running away whilst Tali and Marcus lamely dangled a piece of cardboard in the air. They managed to perform only two readings out of at least thirty attempts.

The moral of this story is very simple: to introduce tarot to the world, we need to overcome its already damaged reputation.

In this concluding chapter, we will examine how we face the world with our tarot. This is where we must generalise widely and point you toward further resources, for the attitude toward tarot varies from place to place and time to time. There are phases and places when and where tarot is popular and widely acknowledged; at other times, interest among the general public seems to wane. We think that, at the present time, all it would take is one celebrity to endorse the cards for a massive upsurge in interest to take place. Whether this would be a good or a bad thing is hard to say, so we will not go there!

However, based on our long experience of teaching and working with tarot readers worldwide, we can suggest some useful general methods of presenting tarot to the whole world, should you wish to, or to use if find yourself in a position where you have to make such a presentation.

Your Tarot Face

Our first, most basic suggestion deals with the face or persona you present when you describe tarot to other people out there in the big wide world. Whether they are friends, family, work colleagues, or even hard-nosed journalists out for a story, we must show them a tarot face that is authentic, original, and perfectly transparent. Indeed, our tarot face must be nonapologetic and totally normal. It must not be hidden—unless for the express sake of mystery, marketing, or play—as there is enough hidden already in the symbols of the cards.

We've all been asked at some time or another what we do or what our interests are. At this point, our tarot face must be in place if we intend to discuss the cards—and, as authentic, spiritually aware folk, it really should be the same face that we show at any other time. We do not believe that tarot is an agent of evil, a curse-related tool, or a means of summoning spirits (well, maybe a little of the latter, but that's beyond the scope of this book). So let us not act as if it actually *is* any of these things.

Elevator Tarot

We mentioned the idea of the "elevator pitch" earlier in this book. Here is your opportunity to develop your own.

An elevator pitch is used in business by project managers or sales managers if someone asks about their work—it's a short and snappy description of what they are doing or selling, which they could deliver in the time it takes an elevator to move between two or three floors. Similarly, we believe that you should prepare an elevator pitch for a few aspects of tarot, so that you can professionally and confidently face these questions when they inevitably arise.

We will share a few of the likely questions and our particular responses. You may choose to design your own, to be absolutely authentic; you may also want to generate a few variations for use with different audiences.

What is Tarot?

Tarot is the term given to a deck of cards that usually comprises seventy-eight images. It arose in Italy almost six hundred years ago and has been used ever since for fortunetelling, inspiration, and self-discovery. For a long time, it was wrongly associated with superstition and spirits; however, since the 1960s, tarot has been going through a revival with about a thousand different decks currently in publication.

How Does Tarot Work?

There is no definitive answer to this. However, we believe that tarot works by illustrating the patterns of life, which are all connected. The difficult thing is to learn to interpret the cards' symbols in a meaningful and useful way. When the cards are shuffled and laid down, we believe they can reflect anything that is going on in the universe, including all possible futures.

What's the Most Interesting Question You Have Ever Been Asked?

Marcus was once asked to read for a photojournalist who was undergoing a crisis of faith in her work. The reading encouraged her to take a slightly new approach to her work, which later resulted in a widely reported uncovering of a scandal situation.

What's the Most Memorable Tarot Reading You Have Ever Done?

Tali once gave what seemed like an entirely negative reading for a client; however, at the end of the reading, he said that it had helped him decide not to commit suicide that night, as he had originally planned. This gave her the insight that tarot can demonstrate to people that their life is part of a bigger picture—a connected universe.

So Can You Tell My Future?

We can read the cards for you and would be happy to do so. We charge for it, and a reading lasts about an hour. We can provide our website address and client testimonials, if you like. We're happy to answer any questions you may have.

Have You Ever Had Anyone for Whom You Couldn't Read the Cards?

We have both had a few people who remained totally poker-faced throughout the whole reading, said very little, and didn't give anything away when they left the table. It's hard to know for sure if they were doing this because they were scared, or playing "test the reader," or for some other reason. This made them difficult to read for. Sometimes we get an absolute blank from the cards and have to decline the reading at that particular moment; however, there is no one we haven't been able to read for at all.

I'm Really Surprised You Are Interested in Tarot; You Seem Like a Rational Person Otherwise

For this comment we present two very different responses:

Marcus: Well, I've been interested in tarot for thirty years now. In that time I've raised a family, moved house, worked in several moderately successful careers, and earned a number of academic awards, including an MBA. I don't see anything irrational with tarot, since you can appreciate it on so many levels. I think a majority of other people see it as being connected with superstitions, which are not actually part of tarot as I experience it. Would you like a reading with me?

Tali: Really? Me, rational? (with a shrug of the shoulders)

Knowing What You Are Talking About

Over three decades, we've had plenty of experiences such as talking to a group of people about quantum physics and its relationship to tarot, only to discover a real quantum mathematician in the audience, or talking to a group of people about "our new idea" in tarot, only to discover three of them have been using it for ten years because we all actually got it out of a Mary K. Greer book at least fifteen years ago. This has taught us to only talk about what we know. The world is a surprisingly smaller place than we think. For instance, only a week prior to writing this, Marcus was teaching a class and referred to a reasonably obscure psychologist, only to find that someone in the class was one of his personal students. Luckily for Marcus, the student provided him with a comprehensive reading list and a personal introduction to the man following the class!

So our advice here is: only talk about what you know, and know what you're talking about. Never be tempted to stray into arguable territory or pursue vague points. We have provided in the reading list a few recommended titles on the history of tarot. If you are going to present tarot to others, please do spend a little time getting your facts straight. The reality of tarot is often even more fascinating than the myths and stories.

Legal and Other Worldly Concerns

There are four general areas of concern into which the practice of tarot falls, in common with any other trade or practice.

- Legal
- Commercial/trade
- Advertising
- Media (print, broadcast, Internet)

Firstly, we should mention here that nothing in this book is to be construed as legal advice. However, we believe that, in the UK and Europe, the legal and commercial issues are fairly straightforward in practice, and they do not expressly mention tarot. Suppose that you claim to channel Zathras from the planet Zog, your client accepts this (and is not in a "vulnerable" state), you charge $1,000 for doing so, and you mention that you do not offer refunds. The client agrees. Then you channel Zathras, but the client is unhappy with the message and raises a complaint. Unfortunately for that client, this situation is highly unlikely to be found illegal (in our opinion—like any legal issue, it is the court that decides). The deciding factor is the clarity of the communication of the conditions of trade, and the agreement between the parties.

The issues of promoting or presenting tarot in the media are somewhat more complex, since in the UK there are important differences between broadcast and print media (and, in some cases, between different areas of media, e.g., commercial and public service). Each has its own unique rules and each has tarot covered unevenly in different areas of the guidance.

We recommend you consult our guide at http://www.fortunetell-inglaws.com/ for these issues, or for non-UK readers, use the guide as an outline of the likely areas your local legislation will cover, and go discover them.

With regard to advertising in the UK, there is a body covering all advertising, whether print or broadcast, and its rules are very clear and commonsensical—no advertising that you can cure warts with your cards, for example, at least not in the UK.

In the UK, you do not have to state that your services are "for entertainment purposes only." In fact, when we researched these legislations two years ago, we were told by a legal representative that to do so would actually form a binding contract of your services. Thus, if you gave a really profound, moving, life-changing, and accurate reading, the client could later that week decide to sue you. Your reading was contracted specifically for "entertainment" and the client was not "entertained." Whether that would hold up in court, we do not know; however, our recommendation has always been simply not to state something that you do not have to state.

Note that we have not said anything about ethics. The simple fact is that many readers confuse a "statement of ethics" with legal trading terms and conditions, or else they state "ethics" that are actually not required nor practical to anybody. Such a statement is usually stated in the negative—much like walking into your doctor's office and seeing a big sign saying, "I hold the intention not to harm you," which would be somewhat alarming as well as unnecessary.

You may decide to join a tarot organisation that can guide you toward a proper statement of professional conduct, ethics, and practice. However, it is an unregulated area of practice, aside from the legal, commercial, and marketing issues we have already mentioned, so a code of practice or ethics is more for your benefit, as a sort of framework, rather than being of any use to your clients.

Tarot and Your Family: Coming Out

When we share with our nearest and dearest something that means a lot to us, we have a desire for them to be happy for us and to support us in whatever we wish to do in life. However, we all know that this is not as easy as it sounds. Not everybody in your life will support and respect your beliefs, or how you choose to live your life, on issues ranging from sexuality to religion to whom you spend your time with. Shakespeare so wisely wrote, "To thine own self be true," but we would paraphrase this as "to thine own self *and set of values* be true."

When you share with some people the fact that you are into tarot, their response may be shock, horror, or just a simple frown. There is a "coming out" process with tarot—deciding to tell or not to tell, and if you do decide to tell, what is the best way to go about it. There are a lot of considerations to take into account, but the first thing to remember is do not be apologetic—you do not have to justify your interest in tarot, full stop.

Okay, suppose you've decided to tell your friends and family. Let's look at how to go about this. Nobody knows your friends and family better than you do; the question, however, is how well do they know you? Are you one of those people who has spent most of their life trying to please other people, and to fit into their perceived notions of what you are? If this is the case, you need to look at this behaviour before anything else. Maybe your love of tarot has come at a time when you are realising that you need to be true to what you believe in, and not what other people think. You are unique (just like everybody else!), and your love of tarot is part of you, as much as that quirky little smile you may have, or your laugh that people poke fun at because you sound like a hiccupping donkey.

So let's put this into perspective, folks—if people around you are not going to like your interest in tarot, they will just have to get over it, because tarot is a part of you that is not defined by anything or anyone else. Just as the images of the major arcana act as symbols to access your deepest self, this issue is about you being true to your deepest yourself. We spend our lives conforming to the expectations of others and the roles we fulfill at home and at work, and it often takes many years before we are comfortable releasing ourselves from these expectations.

However, just as you have every right to express what you believe in, you also have every right to keep your beliefs to yourself, if that is what you wish to do. In your working life, for instance, you may feel that it is inappropriate and irrelevant for you to share details of your personal life. Only discuss your private life when you are ready and the circumstances are right. The timing should always be in your hands only, being more Temperance and less the Chariot—it is up to you.

The High Priestess, the medium of intuition expressing the truth about ourselves, can be recognised in this quote below:

The voice of the authentic self seems to be the same as the intuitive voice, that quiet but persistent voice that whispers new ideas to us in the middle of the night, on vacation, or after meditating. Intuition speaks in short, clear messages that are qualitatively different from the repetitive mind chatter that makes us feel anxious. Intuition tells us where the authentic choice is—for us. (Carol Adrienne, Ph.D.)[33]

Tarot and the Art of War

The book known as *The Art of War,* by Sun Tzu, may initially seem to have little to do with tarot, but it contains many interesting approaches to effective communication. Whilst we tarot readers are generally a peace-loving folk, it is not forbidden for us to consult such manuals to gain advantages in our own art and our presentation of it to the world. So let us consider some key concepts from Sun Tzu's classic as well as related texts from the game of Go and the Dark School of Taoism.[34]

When engaging with a cynic from whom you cannot otherwise escape, the first rule is always:

Run Away

However, here are some other useful plans of action.

Steal the Firewood to Kill the Fire

This means being open with others about your interest in tarot reading from the outset. In this way you can take control of the situation; you tell them rather than them telling you. Effectively you are depriving them of the firewood to start the fire.

The Vital Points Are Often the Same for Both Sides

Strip down tarot to the bare bones. For instance, if we say that tarot is a tool for communicating, or that it acts as a trigger for intuition, that is an inarguable fact and also something with which the other person may be able to identify. It is a common rule of polite diplomacy to always find the common denominator in any tricky area of communication.

Leisurely Watch the Campfires from Across the River, or Relax on the Mountain, Watching the Tigers Fight Below

This is the strategy of allowing people to argue amongst themselves without getting dragged into the argument. If you are with a group of people and there appears to be no way of getting out of a ridiculous argument (and this goes for anything, not just tarot), adopt this strategy and ask one person what they think of another person's comments. Then ask a third person what they think about the second person's comments. This can be very educational for you, and prevents you from being the focus of attention yourself.

Feign Stupidity Instead of Madness

This is one of our preferred strategies when presented with an argument, as it often proves educational. When someone accuses you in some way because of your interest in tarot, it is best to feign stupidity and draw out the actual reasoning behind the argument, rather than to try to defend it from an angry position.

This approach also works for other negative attacks. When Marcus was recently the recipient of a "curse" e-mail, he simply responded to the person to thank them and ask them if they would kindly explain the nature of the curse, as it was one he had not come across before. Needless to say, the person was unable to reply—how would they?—thus binding them with their own negativity.

Facing Up to Six Types of Attitude

There are six types of attitudes that we may come across in regard to how tarot is perceived by others.[35] These attitudes became apparent after focus groups were set up to assess how people perceive religious and alternative practices in the media to determine the varying degrees of acceptability. If we as tarot readers and learners are aware of people's limits of belief, we can adjust our responses and lessen the negative reaction we may receive from being open about tarot.

The particular case study, whilst perhaps somewhat limiting, identified six groups. Each of them requires a different presentation.

- Vulnerable people
- Acceptors
- Frightened Rejecters
- Scientific Rejecters
- Don't Knows
- Experts

We would never read for "vulnerable" people, as they—by definition—already have issues to deal with in their life. This category includes someone suffering from schizophrenia or any other debilitating mental illness, for example. It also includes people who are drunk or under the influence of drugs at the time of reading, which calls for an outright refusal to read for them.

Acceptors and Experts are on the other end of the spectrum; the danger here is overdoing the delivery, such as making excuses for tarot or giving explanations that do not need to be made. It is far better to ask the other person what they already know and feel about tarot and letting their responses dictate how you engage with them.

The Frightened Rejecters are interesting because here we can learn much about what has gone wrong with the perception of tarot in society. It is worth adopting a curious and enquiring approach to such people, and being genuinely and nonjudgmentally interested in what they have to say. We would never dismiss their fears or argue about them; instead, we would look to see what aspects of their fear are based on evidence, and then see if we could provide good countering examples, or query the interpretation of the evidence. It is no use trying to argue with someone who is frightened of tarot with good reason—perhaps because they experienced an upsetting or unprofessional reading, or have strong religious beliefs about all aspects of "the occult" (more on that below).

The Scientific Rejecters are also interesting because they provide an opportunity to refine our own ideas about tarot. We can discuss the nature of science, psychology, and philosophy and how those fields impact contemporary tarot practice. Any discussion should be approached as a learning experience.

We should also note that most modern scientists working in cosmology and quantum physics cheerily accept that they really do not know what is actually going on; they are just attempting to arrive at the most comprehensive, consistent, and congruent model of reality. Our response is that tarot provides us with such a model, in metaphor rather than formula.

When dealing with the Don't Knows, we must be careful not to be evangelical about our interest and resist any attempt to "convert" them to a member of Cult Tarot or Tarot-holics Anonymous. Our interest in tarot should be part of a wide range of activities and interests, not an obsession or our entire focus in life. The Don't Know is often a "don't care," and it is not our job to automatically attempt to convert people to tarot or any other cause.

The Problem of "the Occult"

The feedback given indicated that there are two labels used to describe esoteric subjects: either "psychic" or "occult." It is the perception of differences between the two camps that makes one seem more acceptable than the other.

"Psychic" disciplines such as astrology, mediumship, and faith healing were perceived as being more mainstream and thus were seen as no threat. They were felt to be positive and beneficial to one's well-being, rather than malevolent in nature. However, the more the subject touched upon exerting influence over one's mind, the more it was deemed unacceptable and to be treated with caution.

At the other extreme, subjects such as Satanism, black magic, and voodoo were instantly recognised as being "occult" and taboo. They were perceived as being sinister and detrimental to well-being, verging on being too dangerous to be exposed to, in any shape or form.

So where does tarot fall between these two camps? The research showed that it is generally perceived as being somewhere in the middle—in other words, being neither fish nor fowl. This leads us to believe that tarot can be very tricky for people to accept, since it can neither be rejected straight-out nor accepted into the mainstream. If you are to present tarot to others, you should be aware that you may have to verbally "slide it up" the scale of acceptability in the majority of cases, sometimes all the way from it being considered as "evil" as Satanism.

Presenting Tarot in Context

When presenting tarot to the world, one must be aware of context and expectations as well as perceptions. Tarot readings performed at a gala ball or at a science-fiction convention are likely to be received in very different manners—and sometimes not in the manner you might expect. For instance, we have Christian friends who use tarot as a tool for prayer and contemplation, and also know of others who consider it the work of the devil.

So it is always best to present tarot by first asking about the person or group's previous knowledge of the subject. A simple question like "I'm interested to learn what you guys know (or think) about Tarot" is sufficient to establish some broad boundaries. It will also usually uncover easy routes of explanation and interest—for example, "It's used with ouija boards" and "I had a tarot reading done once and it was quite accurate" both provide interesting paths to explore.

So please do not assume that a science-fiction fan will be interested in tarot, or that an attendee at a gala ball would not be interested. If you maintain an open mind to the possibilities, you may be surprised at the outcomes of performing tarot introductions or readings.

Tarot as a Means of Empowerment

We believe that people should be empowered by coming into contact with tarot; at its best, it can be a tool of self-empowerment and self-development, with the user very much in the driving seat. Thus we also believe it's best to present tarot to the world in such a way that it's not perceived as exerting any unwanted influence on people, which might take them out of their personal comfort zone.

As Abraham Maslow said, "He that is good with a hammer tends to think everything is a nail." The more we can help people to see that tarot and other esoteric disciplines are part of the "empowerment and development tool kit," the more people will be able to see beyond their preconceptions. The emphasis needs to be put on the tarot being positive and transformative, an enabler rather than a pacifier. People do not want to be made to feel vulnerable, or to experience something out of their control. A tarot reading should be about the client gleaning his or her own solutions through the reader's interpretation of the cards.

Here are some wise words from the solution-oriented approach of psychologist Steve de Shazer:

• Acceptance should be unconditional.

• The client has everything needed to solve the problem.

- The only difficulty is that clients do not know that they know how to solve their problems.
- Problem talk creates problems. Solution talk creates solutions.

If you are working in a more engaged and dynamic way with your client, here are two useful questions to pose, also drawn from de Shazer's work. They are particularly applicable if you have established a multisession approach for your work together:
- "What are your best hopes for our work together?"
- "How will you know when you are experiencing your best hopes or making progress toward them?"

Facing Divinatory Moments

We stand before the wonder of the world, and we feel the great mystery deep in our bones. The enigma of our living and our dying calls out to us; we feel the evanescence of our bodies, we search for meaning and purpose on a fragile bridge over the nothingness of unknowing. (Dr. Eitan Fishbane)

At some time in our tarot journey, we all experience a reading that confirms for us that there is something way beyond ourselves at work in our lives. This happened to Marcus and Tali when they were hired to do readings for an event. We had read for a long line of querents and we were about to finish for the evening. We were then asked by the organiser to do one last reading for her friend, who had been too frightened to have a reading, but really wanted one. Tali was asked by Marcus to comment on a single-card reading for this very nervous, elderly querent. She found herself speaking about the Wheel of Fortune card and experienced a strange coincidence, since she had had a virtually identical hospital experience and medical condition as the querent.

The querent had asked, "Why was I saved?" and it was a profound experience for Tali to consider this synchronicity as a call to answer, "So that you can tell others the world is bound by invisible knots"—in other words, that we are all part of a hidden story bigger than ourselves. For Tali, the experience was confirmation that our work is on the right path to awaken people to a considered use of tarot that has real impact on our lives—as Marcus says, "Tarot to engage life, not escape it."

Exploring Tarot Online

There are many opportunities to explore tarot online. We recommend our own social network, Tarot-Town.com, as a convenient portal into the Internet world of tarot, as well as Llewellyn Worldwide's website, www.llewellyn.com, which contains links to a good range of resources.

A basic search will show you many hundreds of tarot blogs; however, only a comparatively small number are kept regularly updated. You can search Twitter for tarot-related feeds, although many are endless and automatic "card of the day" systems. You may also be interested in the many high-quality and fascinating podcasts that are available, often featuring interviews with leading speakers, authors, artists, and teachers of tarot, including the fantastic *Beyond Worlds* radio show at www.tarottribe.com.

One of the main obstacles to tarot development in the "real world" is the ability to practice. We heard recently from our Tarot House in Hong Kong that whilst there was a whole cohort of stellar students, all of them had balked at providing readings for the general public and thus were stuck practising on each other—with the danger of feeling that they didn't know quite enough to help each other develop. The Internet presents a solution to this dilemma by offering many forums and online groups where you can practice your readings in a supportive environment. At least one of these, Tarot-Town.com, has video chat so you can practice virtually face to face. You can also begin to offer paid readings on a system such as Shindig Tarot (www.shindigtarot.com), which features face to face video chat along with an innovative online deck and virtual cards that can be shuffled, spread, and read just like the real thing. See Appendix One for more resources.

The history of tarot is still being written and will continue to develop as people continue to embrace it as a valid and authentic system of Western spirituality and insight. It can be appreciated purely as art, as a psychological tool, or as a mystical means of revelation. In its endless variations, it will continue to entwine itself in human awareness.

We invite you to consider how you will come face to face with tarot in your everyday life. We hope that we have provided you with some ideas on how to answer this question as you progress on your lifetime journey through the cards. We'll leave you with our tarot blessing: May a full deck of possibilities be yours.

Glossary

Bridging: The skill of visually and/or intuitively connecting the symbols of the cards in a way that makes sense in the context of the reading.

Chunking: The level of detail by which a person represents the world to themselves. This can be detailed or big picture.

Clean language: A technique to clarify a situation through the use of metaphorical language, designed to minimize the impact of a person's conscious interpretations or assumptions.

Coded questions: An esoteric method by which inner visualised characters are presented coded questions whose meaning is unknown to the visualiser. This allows for the inner characters to be "tested" without the conscious response of the visualiser.

Elevator pitch: A short description of something suitable to be delivered to someone between a couple of floors of elevator journey. It is a business term for ensuring you have your project or product neatly summarised in case you meet someone important in the elevator.

Flat spreads: A standard spread which simply uses positions of cards on a table.

Future significator: A card chosen to represent who you want to be, not who you are now. It allows for more complex spreads.

Gated spread: A unique Tarosophy method which links several spreads that can only be read by feeding into them questions suggested by activity carried out as a result of the previous spread. It engages the real life of the participant chained together by tarot leading to profound insight. See www.gatesoftarot.com for Gated Spreads occurring during the year.

Geographical spread: A spread which lays out cards around a larger space than a table, such as around the house.

House (astrology): The context by which planets may be seen in an astrological chart.

Inner critic: Our conscious, thinking mind, prone to criticism and analysis.

Installation: The method by which practicing skills imprints them into your subconscious mind.

Language marker: A word or pattern of words that indicates a deeper aspect of unconscious processing. An example would be the word "see," which marks that you are actually "seeing" something inside your head, as in "I see what you mean".

Layered spread: A spread which uses cards placed on top of previous cards in the spread.

Linking words: The words which allow us to continue a communication without forming a complete sentence such as "and," "or," "whilst," etc.

Navigating: The skill of talking to and about our deck.

Nonpositional spread: A spread in which the cards themselves, rather than their positions, denote their meaning in the overall interpretation.

Pinpointing: The skill of intuitively locating the physical centre or key symbol of an individual card.

Planchette: The wooden pointer used on a Ouija board.

Ripple spread: A card layout scheme that shows the ramifications of a particular choice or choices and how those choices are interconnected with each other.

Sigil: A symbol which embodies (in magical practice) a unique spirit or energy.

Significator: The card in a spread that represents the person asking the question or getting the reading.

Spirit catcher: A shamanic device that captures a local spirit, sometimes in a net.

Split deck: Separating out different parts of the deck (e.g., all the major arcana cards, or all the minor arcana cards, or all the court cards) for use in a reading.

Soul mate: The "other half" of one's soul, the perfect partner. According to Plato, all beings were once both male and female, and were split apart in the past. The soul mate is our missing half.

Appendix One:
Online Resources

To learn more about the many innovative techniques featured in this book, we invite you to become a member of **Tarot Professionals** through our national Tarosophy® Tarot Association—for students, newcomers, and experienced tarot readers—at www.tarotprofessionals.com. Membership includes a subscription to the world's leading tarot magazine, *Tarosophist International*, now with over a thousand pages of quality tarot articles, insights, and methods, as well as access to Tarot-City (www.tarotcity.com), which contains premium content, news, videos, and regular updates. Tarot Professionals hosts an annual Tarosophy® Conference in the beautiful Lake District of England, attended by such luminaries as Rachel Pollack, Lon Milo DuQuette, and many others. As a free service to the tarot community, Tarot Professionals also provides a growing worldwide database of legislation, laws, and statutes with regard to "fortunetelling" and tarot at www.fortunetellinglaws.com. You can meet and make friends in your area through one of our friendly Tarosophy® Tarot

Houses; learn more at www.mytarothouse.com)\. If you are interested in a comprehensive course of tarot studies, we offer a range of choices, from beginner to advanced. Our flagship course is the online **Hekademia Tarot Course**, a two-year, degree-style program delivered with the latest learning technology, which features one-on-one supervision by Marcus Katz. You can see the details at www.tarosophyuniversity.com.

Tarot-Town, our thriving social network of tarot students and enthusiasts, can be found at www.tarot-town.com. Join thousands of "tarot townsfolk" in a vast range of activities, projects, and discussions, with video classes, gated spreads, and free guides taking tarot education to whole new levels.

For social networking with other tarot enthusiasts worldwide, join us on **Facebook** at http://www.facebook.com/groups/tarotprofessionals/ or search "Tarot Professionals" on Facebook. You can catch our Twitter feed at @The Tarosophist or http://twitter.com/TheTarosophist.

For comments on this book, updates, and more, see http://www.tarotfacetoface.com.

You may also be interested in **The Tarot Review** (www.thetarotreview.com), our peer-reviewed, professionally edited site for considered and practical reviews of tarot decks.

For tarot book lovers, please call by the **Tarot Book Club** at www.tarotbookclub.com, hosted by Nadine Roberts. There you can see reviews, recommendations, and author interviews for all the latest releases in the world of tarot books.

Tarot Professionals supports Den Elder's **World Tarot Day**™ (May 25) at http://www.worldtarotday.com (now World Tarot Week®—a week-long celebration of the diversity of divination!), and the **Tarosophy Tarot Symposium** (http://www.tarotsymposium.com), which both aim to raise awareness of tarot in contemporary society and bring together tarot readers worldwide.

For courses in the Western esoteric initiatory traditions, alchemy, Kabbalah, witchcraft, tarot, apprenticeship, inner guide meditation, Thelema, and the Hermetic Order of the Golden Dawn, visit the **Far Away Centre** at http://www.farawaycentre.com.

For more innovative and thoughtful tarot at the leading edge and beyond, please visit our friends and partners:

Tali's Tarot Speakeasy Blog (http://www.tarotspeakeasy.com)

Rachel Pollack (http://www.rachelpollack.com)

Mary K. Greer (http://marygreer.wordpress.com)

Dr. Art Rosengarten (http:// www.moonlightcounseling.com)

Lon Milo DuQuette (http://www.lonmiloduquette.com)

James Wells (http://jameswells.wordpress.com)

Enrique Enriquez (http://tarology.wordpress.com)

Magicka School (http://www.magickaschool.com)

Emily Carding's Transparent Tarot (http://www.childofavalon.com)

Adam McLean's Tarot Art and Decks
(http://www.alchemywebsite.com/tarot)

Lyn Birkbeck's Astrology (http://www.lynbirkbeck.com)

Tarot by Phil (http://www.tarotbyphil.com)

Tero Hynynen (http://www.tarotpuu.com)

The House of Life (http://www.thehouseoflife.co.uk)

Mike Hernandez (http://www.justenoughtarot.com)

Stella Luna (http://thetarotreader.com.au)

Beyond Worlds Radio Show (http://www.tarottribe.com)

Theresa Reed, The Tarot Lady (http://www.thetarotlady.com)

Tarot of the Sevenfold Mystery
(http://thealchemicalegg.com/Tarot.html)

Appendix Two:
Reading Lists by Chapter

Chapter 1—Face to Face with Your Deck:
Essential Skills and Methods

Gray, Eden. *Mastering the Tarot*. New York: NAL, 1973.

Greer, Mary K. *Tarot Reversals*, St. Paul, MN: Llewellyn, 2001.

———. *21 Ways to Read a Tarot Card*. Woodbury, MN: Llewellyn, 2007.

Huggens, Kim. *Tarot 101*. Woodbury, MN: Llewellyn, 2010.

Katz, Marcus, and Tali Goodwin. *Tarot Flip*. Keswick, UK: Forge Press, 2010.

———. *Tarot Twist*. Keswick, UK: Forge Press, 2010.

Louis, Anthony. *Tarot Plain and Simple*. St. Paul, MN: Llewellyn, 2003.

Michelson, Teresa. *The Complete Tarot Reader*. St. Paul, MN: Llewellyn, 2005.

Pollack, Rachel. *Seventy-Eight Degrees of Wisdom*. London: Thorsons, 1997.

Quinn, Paul. *Tarot for Life*. Wheaton, IL: Theosophical Publishing House, 2009.

Thomson, Sandra A. *Pictures from the Heart*. New York: St. Martin's Griffin, 2003.

Waite, A. E. *The Key to the Tarot*. Sydney: Century Hutchinson, 1989.

Warwick-Smith, Kate. *The Tarot Court Cards: Archetypal Patterns of Relationship in the Minor Arcana*. Rochester, VT: Destiny Books, 2003.

Chapter 2—Face to Face with Your Deck: Practicing Tarot

Abraham, Sylvia. *How to Use Tarot Spreads*. St. Paul, MN: Llewellyn, 1997.

Bunning, Joan. *Learning Tarot Spreads*. San Francisco: Red Wheel/ Weiser, 2007.

Burger, Evelin, and Johannes Fiebig. *Complete Book of Tarot Spreads*. New York: Stirling, 1997.

Fiorini, Jeanne. *Tarot Spreads and Layouts*. Atglen, PA: Shiffer Publishing Ltd., 2010.

Konrad, Sandor. *Classic Tarot Spreads*. Atglen, PA: Schiffer Publishing, 1985.

Michelson, Teresa. *Designing Your Own Tarot Spreads*. St. Paul, MN: Llewellyn, 2003.

Naylor, A.R. *Tarot Abecedarian: The Treasure House of Images*. Thame, UK: Mandrake Press, 1997.

Vogler, Christopher. *The Writer's Journey*. Studio City, CA: Michael Wiese Productions, 2007.

Chapter 3—Facing the Questions

Meyer, Martin, and Richard Smith. *Ancient Christian Magic.* New York: HarperCollins, 1994.

Chapter 4—Facing the Querent

Bruit-Zaidman, Louise, and Pauline Schmitt-Pantel. Trans. Paul Cartledge. *Religion in the Ancient Greek World.* Cambridge: Cambridge Press, 1994.

Illes Johnston, Sarah. *Ancient Greek Divination.* Chichester, UK: Wiley-Blackwell, 2008.

Vandenberg, Phillip. *Mysteries of the Oracles: The Last of the Secret Antiquity.* London: Tauris, 2007.

Chapter 5—Facing the Crowd: Reading for Parties and Groups

There are surprisingly few books dealing specifically with group activities and party games with tarot. You may be interested in *The Tarot Game* by Jude Alexander (Schiffer, 2011), which provides a "tarot-lite" board game for groups. You may also consult any book of party games and modify the ideas to tarot as we have done here.

Chapter 6—Facing the Outside World: Tarot for Engaging Life

Bates, Bryan. *The Way of Wyrd.* London: Hay House, 2005.

Carr-Gomm, Philip. *The Elements of the Druid Tradition.* Shaftesbury, UK: Element, 1991.

Castenda, Carlos. *The Teachings of Don Juan: A Yaqui Way of Knowledge.* New York: Pocket Books, 1986.

Fries, Jan. *Visual Magick: A Manual of Freestyle Shamanism.* Oxford: Mandrake, 1992.

Jayanti, Amber. *Living the Tarot*. St. Paul, MN: Llewellyn, 1993.

Lorelei, Lady. *Tarot Life Planner*. London: Bounty Books, 2005.

McElroy, Mark. *Putting the Tarot to Work*. St. Paul, MN: Llewellyn, 2004.

Pollack, Rachel. *The Forest of Souls: A Walk through the Tarot*. St. Paul, MN: Llewellyn, 2003.

Chapter 7—Facing Each Other: Tarot and Relationships

Fairfield, Gail. *Choice-Centered Relating and the Tarot*. York Beach, ME: Samuel Weiser, 2000.

Johnson, Robert A. *We: Understanding the Psychology of Romantic Love*. San Francisco: Harper and Row, 1983.

Laurence, Theodore. *The Sexual Key to the Tarot*. New York: Citadel Press, 1971.

Schwartz-Salant, Nathan. *The Mystery of Human Relationship*. New York: Routledge, 2005.

Tennov, Dorothy. *Love and Limerence: The Experience of Being in Love*. New York: Stein and Day, 1981.

Chapter 8—Facing Yourself: Tarot for Self-Discovery

Anonymous. *Meditations on the Tarot*. Shaftesbury, UK: Element Books, 1991.

Banzhaf, Hajo. *Tarot and the Journey*. York Beach, ME: Samuel Weiser, 2000.

Echols, Signe E., Robert Mueller, Ph.D., and Sandra A. Thomson. *Spiritual Tarot: Seventy-Eight Paths to Personal Development*. New York: Avon Books, 1996.

Fairfield, Gail. *Choice Centered Relating and Tarot.* York Beach. ME: Samuel Weiser, 2000.

Gad, Irene. *Tarot and Individuation.* Berwick, ME: Nicholas Hays, 2004.

Gardber, Richard. *Evolution Through the Tarot.* New York: Samuel Weiser, 1977.

Gwain, Rose, *Discovering Yourself through the Tarot: A Jungian Guide to Archetypes and Personality.* Rochester, VT: Destiny Books, 1994.

Hamaker-Zondag, Karen. *Tarot as a Way of Life.* York Beach, ME: Samuel Weiser, 1997.

Jette, Christine. *Tarot Shadow Work.* St. Paul, MN: Llewellyn, 2000.

Jodorowsky, Alejandro. *The Way of Tarot: The Spiritual Teacher in the Cards.* Rochester, VT: Destiny Books, 2004.

Lee Braden, Nina. *Tarot for Self Discovery.* St. Paul, MN: Llewellyn, 2002.

Pollack, Rachel. *Tarot Readings and Meditations.* Wellingborough, UK: Aquarian Press, 1986.

Rosengarten, Arthur. *Tarot and Psychology: Spectrums of Possibility.* St. Paul, MN: Paragon House, 2000.

Sargent, Carl. *Personality, Divination, and the Tarot.* London: Rider and Co., 1998.

Summers, Catherine, and Julian Vayne. *Personal Development with the Tarot.* London: Quantum, 2002.

Walter Stirling, Stephen. *Tarot Awareness: Exploring the Spiritual Path: Correspondences, Meditations, and Guided Visualizations.* St. Paul, MN: Llewellyn, 2000.

Woudhuysen, Jan. *Tarot Therapy: A Guide to Your Unconscious.* Los Angeles: J. P. Tarcher, 1979.

Chapter 9—Facing All Fronts: Twelve Spreads

Birkbeck, Lyn. *The Watkins Astrology Handbook: The Practical System of DIY Astrology*. London: Watkins Books, 2006.

Frawley, John. *The Horary Text Book*. London: Apprentice Books, 2005.

———. *The Real Astrology*. London: Apprentice Books, 2000.

Levine, Stephen. *A Year to Live: How to Live This Year as if It Were Your Last*. New York: Crown Publishing, 1998.

Parker, Julia, and Derek Parker. *K.I.S.S Guide to Astrology*. London: Dorling Kindersley, 2000.

Chapter 10—Tarot in the World

Decker, Ronald, and Michael Dummett. *A History of the Occult Tarot 1870–1970*. London: Duckworth, 2002.

Decker, Ronald, Thierry Depauls, and Michael Dummett. *The Origins of the Occult Tarot*. New York: St. Martin's Press, 1996.

Farley, Helen. *A Cultural History of Tarot: From Entertainment to Esotericism*. London: Tauris, 2009.

Jensen, Frank K. *The Story of the Waite-Smith Tarot*. Croydon Hills, AU: ATS Publications, 2006.

Nichols, Sallie. *Jung and Tarot: An Archetypal Journey*. York Beach, ME: Samuel Weiser, 1984.

O'Neill, Robert. *Tarot Symbolism*. Croydon Hills, AU: ATS Publications, 2004.

Place, Robert M. *The Tarot: History, Symbolism, and Divination*. London: Tarcher Penguin, 2005.

Shotwell, Peter. *Go! More Than a Game*. Tokyo: Tuttle Publishing, 2003.

Endnotes

1. You can watch a video of this student telling us how to read the Three of Pentacles in the future position of a spread in relation to a question about a new relationship—ten minutes into her first-ever tarot class. You will have to join Tarot Professionals to do so at http://www.tarotprofessionals.com/membership.html (accessed August 5, 2011).

2. Neuro-linguistic programming is a range of methods developed in the last thirty years that deal with the way we represent the world inside our head. It is taught to communicators, teachers, counsellors, trainers, salespeople, and anyone who wants to improve their ability to communicate. You can discover more at http://www.nlpmagick.com.

3. Marcus Katz and Tali Goodwin, *Tarot Flip* (Keswick, UK: Forge Press, 2010); Katz and Goodwin, *Around the Tarot in 78 Days* (Woodbury, MN: Llewellyn, 2012).

4. Marcus Katz, *Tarosophy* (Brisbane, AU: Salamander and Sons, 2011).

5. Gérard "Papus" Encausse, *The Tarot of the Bohemians*, ed. A. E. Waite (North Hollywood, CA: Wilshire, 1973), p. 308.

6. This method was first explored in Tali Goodwin's blog, *The Tarot Speakeasy*, at www.tarotspeakeasy.com.

7. The Hermit and the Two of Wands would likely suggest a simple "travel abroad" answer, i.e., do your own thing, by yourself (see most illustrations of the Two of Wands).

8. One place to do so is at the "Around the Tarot in 78 Days" group at http://www.tarot-town.com.

9. Expanded from Marcus Katz and Tali Goodwin, *Tarot Twist* (Keswick, UK: Forge Press, 2011).

10. See Wendy Sullivan and Judy Rees, *Clean Language* (London: Crown House Publishing, 2008).

11. Expanded from Marcus Katz and Tali Goodwin, *Tarot Flip* (Keswick, UK: Forge Press, 2011).

12. An interesting survey of Facebook relationship status changes showed that the most frequent time for such changes—often to "single" from "in a relationship"—is after Valentine's Day, Christmas, and the New Year, and then the vacation period. Such temporal landmarks and reefs in the tides of human affairs often wash people ashore on the island of the tarot reader. "The Right Time for Love," March 2012, https://www.facebook.com/notes/facebook-data-team/the-right-time-for-love-tracking-the-seasonality-of-relationship-formation/10150643989093859.

13. One day we hope to do a survey of tarot readers to determine more specifically how the questions they are asked are related to their environment.

14. See Katz, *Tarosophy*.

15. Tarosophy survey, 2010.

16. There is no particular reason for these numbers other than they are sufficient to get clarity on the situation and are easily remembered. You can, of course, read outwards from the chosen card in both directions in a narrative for as many cards as seems appropriate, even to a full seventy-eight-card reading.

17. To find out more about Enrique, visit his site at www.tarology .wordpress.com/.

18. Leonard Holmes, "Why Your Therapist Is Not Your Friend," About.com, www.mentalhealth.about.com/cs/psychotherapy/a /dualrelshps.htm (accessed March 31, 2012).

19. We highly recommend Mermade Magickal Arts, http://www .mermadearts.com/.

20. Lyn Birkbeck, astrologer, http://www.lynbirkbeck.com.

21. This method was first given in Katz and Goodwin, *Tarot Twist,* and is here presented in an expanded format.

22. For reversals, see Marcus Katz and Tali Goodwin, eds., *Tarot Turn* (Keswick, UK: Forge Press, 2012), which features over 12,000 interpretations of reversed cards by over 140 tarot readers and unique methods of using reversed cards.

23. These extras were derived from Aleister Crowley, *777 and Other Qabalistic Writings* (York Beach, ME: Samuel Weiser, 1982), and David Rankine and Sorita d'Este, *Practical Planetary Magick* (London: Avalonia, 2007).

24. See www.zodiacarts.com/Calendar.shtml (accessed August 4, 2011).

25. For online calculation of your sun and moon signs, you may use the free birth chart function at http://lyn-birkbeck.astro -sites.com.

26. William Shakespeare, *A Midsummer Night's Dream*, Act V, Scene 2.

27. For more on the Inner Guide Meditation Workbook, see http://www.tarotprofessionals.com/innerguide.html.

28. You can join others in carrying out this and many other gated spreads at http://www.tarotprofessionals.com/gates.html.

29. See Katz, *Tarosophy*, the "Fountain of Morpheus" technique.

30. John Frawley, *The Real Astrology* (London: Apprentice Books, 2000), pp. 91–104.

31. Ibid., p. 93.

32. For more about World Tarot Day™ see http://www.worldtarotday .com.

33. Essay on authenticity from Carol Adrienne, available at http://www.caroladrienne.com/en_US/content/view/109/108.

34. Entertainment Survey, Jane Sancho, 2001, http://www.ofcom.org .uk/static/archive/itc/research/beyond_entertainment.pdf.

35. Ibid.

GET MORE AT LLEWELLYN.COM

Visit us online to browse hundreds of our books and decks, plus sign up to receive our e-newsletters and exclusive online offers.

- **Free tarot readings • Spell-a-Day • Moon phases**
- **Recipes, spells, and tips • Blogs • Encyclopedia**
- **Author interviews, articles, and upcoming events**

GET SOCIAL WITH LLEWELLYN

Find us on  🐦 @LlewellynBooks

www.Facebook.com/LlewellynBooks

GET BOOKS AT LLEWELLYN

LLEWELLYN ORDERING INFORMATION

Order online: Visit our website at www.llewellyn.com to select your books and place an order on our secure server.

Order by phone:
- Call toll free within the US at 1-877-NEW-WRLD (1-877-639-9753)
- We accept VISA, MasterCard, American Express, and Discover.

Order by mail:
Send the full price of your order (MN residents add 6.875% sales tax) in US funds plus postage and handling to: Llewellyn Worldwide, 2143 Wooddale Drive, Woodbury, MN 55125-2989

POSTAGE AND HANDLING

STANDARD (US):(Please allow 12 business days)
$30.00 and under, add $6.00.
$30.01 and over, FREE SHIPPING.

CANADA:
We cannot ship to Canada. Please shop your local bookstore or Amazon Canada.

INTERNATIONAL:
Customers pay the actual shipping cost to the final destination, which includes tracking information.

Visit us online for more shipping options. Prices subject to change.

FREE CATALOG!

To order, call
1-877-
NEW-WRLD
ext. 8236
or visit our
website